Fear Not MY CHILD I AM Here

Emerging from the Spiral of Fear

The Practical Mystic's Guide
for Embracing Your Heart's Desire

Carol Lynn Fitzpatrick

Paperback printing, December 2003

ISBN: 0-9742213-0-9

Printed in the United States on acid-free paper

About the Author

 Carol Lynn Fitzpatrick is a group facilitator, presenter and author. Spiritually, she devoted the past 14 years to unraveling the mysteries of a transformation that took her deep into the mystical realms of the Divine. As a result of her experiences, she has co-founded Arayu (ˉa-ra-y-u), a socially conscious organization that delivers spiritual workshops and seminars, involving light, music and contemplative dialog for the purpose of expanding awareness.

As a social activist and organizational change agent, Carol founded River of Light Enterprise, an organization that advocates the empowerment of the individual in systems of governance. She also devoted the better part of the last decade to the community policing movement where she served in a lead marketing role to educate community leaders about the philosophy.

Her interest in creating positive change in people's lives began years ago when she formed a small business, which eventually grew into a design and publishing company that focused on celebrating the human spirit. Carol continues to facilitate transformative change by using her gift of prophesy for healing as she speaks to groups about the choice we are all called to make in the shaping of upcoming world events.

To learn more about Carol's work, access:
www.carolynnfitzpatrick.com
carol@carolynnfitzpatrick.com

*This book is dedicated to
Danielle and James.*

*The Light they bring to the world
inspires me so.*

Fear Not
MY CHILD
I AM HERE

Emerging from the Spiral of Fear

The Practical Mystic's Guide
for Embracing Your Heart's Desire

Carol Lynn Fitzpatrick

Facilitating Transformative Change

P.O. Box 41132
Fredericksburg, Virginia

CONTENTS

CONTENTS

I may not have gone where I intended to go,
but I think I have ended up
where I intended to be.

—Douglas Adams,
Author of *A Hitch-hikers Guide to the Galaxy*

ACKNOWLEDGMENTS

When I think about the road thus far, I feel an overwhelming sense of gratitude for my family and friends who stand witness to my awakening. Their friendship and guidance have enriched my life beyond measure. In particular, I extend a heartfelt thank you to my spiritual family. You know who you are because we have spent many a day, and evening, in the quiet of the moment sharing stories of personal revelations. The learning has been an incredible adventure, and I would not have picked anyone else to learn with but you.

Specifically, when it came to encouraging me to write, or prodding me to dig deeper into the sharing, or simply holding the space to explore the unknown, I owe a special note of thanks to friends Bess, Joan, Malia and Jacquie, and to Vinay.

When it came time to step up to the proverbial plate and speak my truth, the person who has consistently held the space for doing so is a man who warms my heart and shares a deepening love of the Divine with me. He is forever showing me the way by walking his talk. If I had not met Mark Torgeson when I did, I summize that the "out there" idea of putting my experiential learnings to paper would have become just another thought in the halls of wistful thinking.

It was during a meditation that I received the prompting to ask my daughter, Danielle, to serve as editor-in-chief. This was a tall order considering the strained circumstances of our relationship at the time. My decision to follow this inner guidance, and her willingness to accept my offer to work together, is something I will always cherish. The experience of collaborating on this project with someone who shared many of the harsher lessons with me has deepened my appreciation for a wisdom beyond her years. It has also transformed our mother/daughter roles into fellow travelers on the same path.

When it came to questioning the Guide's early information about vibrational frequency and energetic shifting, I quelled my concerns and lack of knowledge on such things by turning to my son James. His explanation of scientific concepts, as relayed to me by the Guides, in simpler terms, prompted me to further research theories of quantum physics and mechanics. His continued encouragement to keep up the writing was also great source of inspiration as we both worked to complete our individual methods of schooling.

Spirit always provides when we are ready, and in this case, it was through a mutual friend that I met Mary Lippitt, a new author whose book turned out to be voted as one of 2002's best. She graciously shared her insights into the world of writing and publishing. Mary served as one of three reviewers of the first, very rough draft, but most importantly, she inspired me to find my voice.

I also wish to thank Terri Singleton who graciously copyproofed the manuscript in its final stages of refinement.

Last but not least, many of the early experiences with the Divine would never have come about had it not been for the steadfast kindness of Asta Michie. As we compelled our mutual teacher, Sri Sathya Sai Baba, to show us the way to opening our hearts more fully to God, she held the sacred space during a particularly fearful time in my life. With steady reassurance, her actions showed me that God never forsakes us.

The great sages, avatars and prophets tell us that in order to realize one's divinity, we are to challenge God to reveal truth to us in every way. We are always to question until we are satisfied, then once we have come to a place of peace, we are to trust and follow our heart rather than the doubting of our mind. Without question, it was my parents who taught me by their steadfast support and unconditional love, even when I could not see it for myself, to muster the courage to begin claiming my birthright.

There is nothing in life to fear,
it is only to be understood.

--- Author Unknown

THE WRITING PROCESS

Aligning with Spirit

There is much talk about listening to our intuition or inner guidance—of talking to God or God speaking to us. In my life, this has been a literal two-way conversation beginning during a particularly fearful time in my life. At first, it was overwhelming to even consider the possibility of God transfiguring my everyday existence, but eventually, in the midst of tending to the details of my *real* life, I began to accept and surrender to the wisdom of a higher power.

The seed for the writing of this book started almost fourteen years ago while in the basement of my home. I was feeling a pressure pushing down onto the top of my head, which was accompanied by an overwhelming sense of a Divine presence. It was so powerful that I felt no desire to resist it. As I surrendered to the intensity of the experience, I felt my internal struggle fall away as this most wondrous, all encompassing expression of Divinity itself infused me with an energetic Light. The experience was transforming. I then heard a voice speak in my mind and was prompted to write. The God presence now within me was clear and unequivocal in the delivery of what I was hearing, feeling and seeing. I did not understand the phenomenon of what was occurring, from a logical standpoint, but trusted it because this brilliant Light was a direct match to the God feeling I have been holding onto from my very earliest remembrances.

With much prompting from Spirit, I have been writing this way nearly every day since that time. Very often, this inner guidance comes over me as a strong knowing. Since that first encounter with God on such a visceral level, I feel that I have been living much of my life backwards. I still have to go through the learning like everyone else does, but Spirit tells me things about myself, my children, those around me and the world at large that are not of the now, but of the past and future probability.

I have come to realize that I am given glimpses of my probable future to keep me on the road to know the Divine more fully and to learn to love unconditionally. In times of strife, my Spiritual Guides have shown me that the only way out of fear is to keep my sights fully focused on the God within me—to pay no attention to the many worldly distractions in life.

If I have chosen to walk the path of transformation in this manner then it has been a process of learning to trust my inner guidance above all else. Since I have set my life goal to realize freedom in every way, I am called to release myself from the many fear-laden beliefs that prohibit me from getting there.

This is a pretty tall order considering that I have allowed fear to shape the better part of my life. It wasn't until I found myself in the midst of a major life crisis that I became aware of just how insidious this feeling had become. When I began surrendering my fears to God, my life started changing for the better. Now this incredible guidance is forever nudging me to follow the inner prompting in an 'instructions on the box' kind of way.

My test always comes as a challenge to follow the intuitive direction I am given or to wallow in the chaos that is brought on by doubt. As with any course of study there comes a time for the final exam. I feel my final exam coming and I may graduate if I have completely transcended the second-guessing of divine will working in my life. Meeting so many gifted spiritual seekers in the same boat, I know I am not alone in this quest to be free of life's stumbling blocks.

Now, as I teach others self-help healing techniques to aid them in their own clearing process, I find that I am not alone in my fear of the unknown. I find that many get stuck and tend to wallow in their fears born from the unconscious choices they have made. The root cause is buying into the illusions of the mind and believing that love is a commodity rather than our natural state of being.

The information you will read about in *Fear Not My Child, I AM Here* is based on real life experiences, but it is also written in co-creation with the spiritual masters and teachers who guide me. There have been many who have taught me over the years, and the lessons were always delivered in the same manner as my first gut-level encounter with God.

The collaboration for this book was with a group of souls who identify themselves as beings of Light or divine masters. They hail from the house of David, representing three generations prior to and including the life of Jesus and his followers. They are Jesus with Daniel and Jacob; Jehosephat, who is the son of David and brother to Jesus; Mary (Jesus' maternal grandmother), who also calls herself the Lady of Compassion.

As an aside, Jesus references his origin not by location but by his affiliation with the Nazarene. The Nazarene were a sect of people in Jewish society who practiced a mystical art form of spirituality. His mastery of the physical realm was the way he saw through the veil of his own understanding at the early age of nine.

Also present is the father of Jacob who says he is not of the house of David because he was born under the sign of Aquarius in the year 1213. Since he is in alignment with the energetic shift that will return in the year 2013, he contributes his knowledge to this work. Sri Sathya Sai Baba, an Avatar who lives in India, serves as master of ceremonies. As my teacher over the years, you will find his wisdom reflected in many of the earlier inspired writings beginning on page 44.

As I move through what now seems like endless days of refining and editing, when a joyful feeling comes over me, I am immediately reminded of Amma, a living Hindu saint who is the embodiment of unconditional love and compassion. She is such a joyful soul and a great source of inspiration.

I give thanks for these Light beings who so freely share their wisdom and deeply touch my heart. Throughout the book, you will find their collective teachings interwoven into the work, but for the sake of keeping it simple, where necessary, I refer to them as *Spiritual Guides* or the *Guides*.

During the months of working on this book, I came to recognize when it was time to write because a timeless state of being would often envelop me. Each time it happened, I felt a most wondrous flowing of energy that transformed me into an altered state, that would then open my field of vision to see, hear and feel the higher knowledge as it was so freely given. Each time, I felt very blessed to receive information this way. As I began to feel the divine current flow through me, my mind quickly moved into a state of neutral. As I relaxed into the moment, I wrote within a feeling of timelessness until the flow of consciousness abruptly stopped, as if to announce the period of learning was complete.

The statements of fact, as they were given to me by the Guides, are related to you just as they were to me. In some cases, I have no way of proving or disproving the information, but where I have access to the latest research, I have included this as further explanation.

As you begin reading, please know that the content, beginning with chapter two, is presented in the order in which it was inspired. Once the writing was complete, I went about organizing the material in what I thought was a logical, linear fashion grouping *like* topics together, but as I did so I kept getting the feeling to stop. I asked if the organization was correct. The Guides answered *no* with instructions on how to reconfigure the chapters.

The explanation for doing so was accompanied by a story. They said, "At first a child is made to walk within his sphere of influence. At first there are baby steps, then there is a time of balancing the concepts of gravity and forward motion. Over time, the child will learn to run and skip and jump with the best of them. First we learn to walk, then to run and eventually we might even learn to dance. It is all in the learning."

As I put the pages back in the order they were written, and proceeded to edit the material from front to back, I remembered why I am always in awe of God. We may not understand the rhyme or reason for the knowledge we are given, but we must trust, simply trust in the learning.

Finally, the sharing of some of the more dramatic 'aha' moments, beginning with chapter one, are revealed for the sake of learning. Where other individuals were involved, I strived to maintain as much privacy as possible without compromising the point of the learning. I honor all individuals who participated in my lessons during this most turbulent time in my life. I feel a tremendous sense of unconditional love and appreciation for the part each played in my awakening.

Please accept this practical guide in the spirit in which it was written, with much love and appreciation for who you are.

—Carol Lynn Fitzpatrick

See nothing;
look at nothing but your goal
ever shining before you.

The things that happen to us do not matter:
what we become through them does.

Every day accept everything
as coming to you from God.

At night,
give everything back into his hands.

—Krishna Yogananda

So Jesus answered and said to them,
"Assuredly, I say to you, if you have faith and do not doubt,
you will not only do what was done to the fig tree,
but also if you say to this mountain,
'Be removed and be cast into the sea,' it will be done.
And whatever things you ask in prayer,
believing, you will receive."

—Matthew 21:21-22

ONE BIG LESSON

*You can look everywhere for answers,
but until you are willing to look inside, you will not
find what you are seeking.*

I realize there are different schools of thought on life, living and the pursuit of happiness but I also must say that all are theories and are no substitution for direct experience. We each have our stories of wanting and waiting for something to happen the way it was taught to us by our parents, teachers, clergy or perhaps an old wise one, but life is meant to be lived in the moment. All learning, from what others tell us, is only relevant and holds value in hindsight of our own experience. This book has been written for this express purpose.

The sharing of my 'aha' moments, found within these pages, provide a narrow slice of learning because it only has to do with me. You will hopefully gain some insight into your own life by reading about what I have learned about mine.

The basis of this body of work was formed from early experience, which then took the better part of my life to shape into a knowing that I am only now unraveling. It has taken time and a deep commitment to come to a place of peace about the choices I made along the way, starting from the time before I was born—yes, before I was born.

It's hard, at first, to realize that we create our reality before we are even born into the physical, but we do. Once the vibrational frequency is chosen and the lessons selected, we make our entry into our family.

I am 49 years old and at this time, I recognize that I have created my world around me. On the soul level, I chose to begin my learning by identifying with the soul-pain of humanity. Looking back to my earliest beginnings, rather than choosing to identify with joy, I chose to identify with the pain and anguish I felt by those around me. By doing so, I held steadfast to a belief in lack and bought into duality (good/bad, light/dark, black/white, love/hate).

These were beliefs I brought into the physical from former life experiences, but were no less a decision on what and how I chose to learn. In fact, even though I recognize much of my choosing now, I am *still* working to integrate this knowing into my physical world.

We each do what works or doesn't work to either affirm or deny our selected path of learning. Whatever decision we make, whether we make it unconsciously or consciously, as we move through life, we are either supported in our choice or are met with resistance.

The important point to understand here, is that my perception of what was occurring in my world, as you will soon read, and the decisions I made that either denied or embraced the Light of God within me, is central to my learning. I believe that it is the core reason why we are all here; to acknowledge and to embrace the God within us.

What is the point of living in the vibration of fear when we are in actuality born as a high vibration of love? I believe the answer to this question is *learning*—learning to love unconditionally.

My adventure, as I set out to understand this basic truth, began when I was born into a family, which at the time, was experiencing much emotional turmoil and financial hardship. Knowing what I know now, this was a perfect entry-point for beginning my awakening process. What better way to learn than to be born into a vibration that both supports and challenges the very qualities in which we resonate.

From a very early age, I remember feeling within me, a brilliant loving, kind Light. Yet, my earliest impression of my physical surroundings was one of being removed, alone, unloved, a burden, forgotten. Now I had no way of understanding the *why* of these divergent feelings, and did not fully understand how my soul set this way of awakening into motion until much later in my life. It wasn't until I had gone through a major upheaval in my mid-thirties, and learned from it, that my eyes began to open to the ways of Spirit.

As I grew older, I came to learn that from 1947 to the late 1950s (I was born in 1954) my parents experienced prolong periods of grief and sadness from the death of immediate family members; first with the tragic passing of my father's two brothers then his father. My maternal grandmother was killed in front of my mother's youngest sister in an act of cold-blooded murder. This event sent my mother into such a state of despair that, in 1959, my father moved the family from Michigan to California.

Needless to say, I was born in the midst of swirling emotions. Now that is not to say that my family of origin was not also happy and busy building a life for themselves; They most certainly were. But the stage was set to experience the vibrations of fear that would play out in my life as recurring themes of grief, anger, resentment, lack, remorse, regret and so forth. So there I went—incarnating into the perfect physical environment that fit the energetic frequencies I was seeking.

I have since learned that the nonverbal transmittal of emotions is a biological function of every human being. It isn't that we just feel our emotions and that's it. Whether we choose to acknowledge or express our feelings, they emit out into the world as electro-magnetic fields. When we are engaged in relationship, our energy fields adjoin with others in a kind of energetic exchange that literally changes the neurobiology of both parties. The same thing occurs not only between two people but with entire groups such as families, friends and communities.

Babies are born as open emotional receivers and whatever they are sensing from their environment, they internalize as they begin building their emotional database about what the world feels like—loving or hostile, kind or mean, inviting or unwanted, happy or sad.

As I began building the internal roadmap of how I would interface with my world, I compared what I was sensing outwardly to that Light I felt inside. In doing so, I took on the belief that the best way to survive and thrive was to keep quiet and to stay out of the fray. As I grew older, I learned to be a helper.

When I was a small child, to more fully immerse myself in this feeling, I would often retreat into the quiet of my mind or seek out of the way places. to escape from the noise and frenzied emotion around me. I'd find places like the inside of a cozy, dark closest or the hollow beneath a willow tree, or in the fields of poppies and tall grasses out out back behind our neighborhood.

As I grew in both age and experience I tuned in less and less to that inner feeling of the Light of God within me, and ever increasingly more to the outside feedback I was receiving as a result of interfacing with my emotional environment.

As I maneuvered my way through childhood, I distinctly remember choosing whether to speak up, or not; to fight back, or not; to act out, or not; to remain quiet and resentful, or not. This decision-making process was in direct alignment (and contrast) to the role I had selected to become a good little girl, to stay quiet and out of the way, to be a helper and a doer.

This chosen role took on twists and turns in my life as I fine-tuned how to protect that inner Light, while also reacting to such outside stimulus as a screaming, angry, aggressive sibling; or perhaps unwanted advances from sexual predators; or distrustful, manipulative individuals.

The choices I made to each of these types of examples resulted in many harsh lessons. In retrospect, with each choice along the way, I can clearly see, in hindsight, when and where I choose silence and defeat over fighting back; resentment over action; stubbornness over wisdom; ignorance over enlightenment; self-denial over empowerment.

As I grew in years, I became so practiced at identifying with what others were feeling, that I began to loose touch with what I wanted *for me*. Instead, I hid behind the many labels of student, teacher, military wife, mother, entrepreneur, et al. I wore these titles like a badge of honor yet inwardly was a scared, insecure little girl who just wanted to be protected.

Instead of honoring my inner guidance, I worked hard to be that outward image I held in my mind's eye by saying, doing and being all the right things for everyone else but myself. Eventually, I became so uncomfortable in my own skin that I began to define myself by what I thought others wanted or expected me to be *for them*. This often played out as in-decisiveness, mind-changing or counter-acting stated intentions as I promised to be everywhere for everyone all at once.

By my late-twenties I had already made many decisions based on a pretty elaborate belief-system born out of perceived hurts, slights and injustices. To be sure, these choices reinforced the constant denial of self, yet I pretended that I had the perfect life with the perfect husband, family, budding career, friends, home life, etc. Nothing could be further from the truth.

The turning point in this cycle of self-deception occurred in my mid-thirties, when my soul said enough of this already. It was time to redirect my life and get right with the Light of God within. By this time, I had so denied my inner voice, at key decision-points along the way, that by the time my life came crashing down around me, there were actually times when I wondered if I was losing touch with God altogether.

I can say now, that I absolutely knew that time was coming; I most certainly saw the signs along the way. The messages and prompts I ignored were like flashing red lights trying to turn me away from the more extreme harshness to come. By that time, fear, self-denial and self-diminishment were such a part of my inner world, there seemed to be no turning back.

There are many nuances to the most dramatic part of my awakening, but for the sake of brevity, I'll begin my example with a medical scare that occurred with my son at age three. After yet another doctor's visit to clear up what was becoming chronic lung congestion, a young military physician tentatively diagnosed him as having cystic fibrosis; but the doctor said it was hard to tell. He just couldn't diagnosis it for sure and told me that James would either outgrow it by around the age of ten or not. I hung onto the words *or not*. It was a nurse who pulled me aside and assured me that she had seen a lot of blond haired babies this way, and her own sons had outgrown the same symptoms. This calmed my worst fears, but I abruptly quit my part-time job.

My boss asked me to keep working, but from home. My innermost desire had always been to stay home and be fully present with my children, without this added pressure, but the better part of me knew I needed to keep paving an economic path, just in case.

The seeds to plan this way were sewn long before my marriage, but became firmly rooted when, on my wedding day, I watched my new husband dance our afternoon away with his old flame. Outwardly, I pretended that all was a happy day, while inwardly, I screamed with the pain of humiliation and anger.

Even as we planned our family, the need to create a way out, if push came to shove, was never an either/or choice with me. No matter what my mind reasoned, my heart forever told me to be prepared, and not just because I loved my craft—I did. But now I was married to a military officer who harbored an endless supply of erratic restlessness, and a future of moving around every few years.

Life in the physical is like this, I think, always working on multiple levels and layers of conscious and unconscious choosing. Decisions born out of hurt and malice never end up in bliss. I was in love with my husband, yet my emotions quietly churned with fear and resentment, which at times actually bordered on hate. Emotionally and energetically, we were a perfect match.

This push-pull way of learning was directly suited to what my soul had set up as my mind constantly went back and forth, back and forth, obsessing over the choices I had made. My now ingrained pattern of choosing not to speak up, or of speaking up and not being heard, repeated itself in every facet of my life. This pattern supplied an endless source of hurt and anger as I inwardly brooded about *everything* in my life, while also holding steadfast to my desire to feel loved and protected.

In the quiet of my mind, I was using the same skills much the same way I had as a child. I would retreat inside myself as I reacted to each perceived hurt or slight, then for days, weeks or even months, brood about it until I had given myself a pep talk to get on with getting on.

About the time my son's health issue had come fully to the surface, my husband decided to start his own business. After taking a 'no money down' seminar, he began purchasing property that required credit cards as financial backup. This was particularly disturbing to me, but in my usual fashion—after endless objections did not deter him—I stuffed my concerns over the voice of reason and swallowed my fear. His reasoning was that I had started my own business so he was starting his.

At this same time, we decided against returning to our home state of California and opted, instead, for raising our children in the Virginia countryside. Being a military family, we knew a decision to put roots down would mean a greater sacrifice.

On Mother's Day, (Spirit giving me a big clue here) we found a farm in the paper and went to take a look. My husband fell in love with the place at first sight. I was overwhelmed by the amount of work we would have to do just to make it livable. The shear size and neglect of the property scared me. I was comfortable in our little townhouse with all the modern conveniences. We had money in the bank and we were on the fast track to pay the mortgage off early.

The new monthly payment seemed formidable. We could not afford it on our income, but it was owner financed, which is what he was looking for. I did not want to pursue the matter and talked endlessly on the pitfalls and drawbacks of diving into such a risky venture. In the end, I quelled my concerns and agreed to making the sellers an offer.

32

It was only after I over-rode the screaming red light signals going off in my gut that I saw a vision. I was shown that if we bought the property, our family would be torn apart and it would be a horrible demise. But there I was, standing in the middle of my modern day kitchen, in spite of my fears, and said "Yes, OK. Let's do it"

I swallowed my concerns and dove in head-on with unbridled enthusiasm. I asked my parents to help us with the down payment, a decision that would come back to haunt me in ways I could never have imagined.

We also quickly learned that in order to purchase the farm and remain in Virginia, my husband would have to serve his next tour of duty in North Carolina.

On a sweltering day in August, my husband, two young children and I moved into an enormous plantation house on 82 acres. It was a 200-year-old farm that had not been fully inhabited for over ten years. It had been left to deteriorate among Mother Nature and was full of snakes, bugs and over-run with mice. There was no way to escape the heat. When winter hit, the old radiator system had to be fixed, and with 52 old, leaky, broken window-panes, the job of plugging the holes just to turn the heat on was mind-boggling.

The first year was both exciting and difficult. We went from a home with modern conveniences to living in the elements. The water was rusty from a well that would eventually muddy up our supply of running water to the point of having to dig a new one. There was always something major to be fixed, or in need of repair. True to the movie out at the time, "The Money Pit," it was all of that and more. Yet, I constantly reminded myself that I was having fun and that we were on a grand adventure.

After eight months, as planned, I became a geographic widow and single parent again. At first it was gut-wrenching, then slowly, as the emotional upheaval of perpetual goodbyes lulled into a strange sort of disheartened normalcy, the marriage began to creak and groan from the stress of prolonged separation. With a stressed out mother and phantom father, the children suffered the consequences all the way around. The stress of living this way became almost unbearable at times.

As the months grew to over a year-and-a-half, the plan was for our family to come together again. Instead, I learned that I was to go it alone *another* year, while he completed an overseas tour of duty.

The day he left was one of the worst days of my life—not because he was leaving—that was bad enough. I began to understand just how much our family finances had deteriorated. Our savings were completely depleted. The two condominiums he had purchased just before we moved to the farm had been sitting empty for months, and to cover the expenses, he had withdrawn money from his credit cards. The stress of raising kids in single-parent mode, fixing an old broken-down farm on my own and building, what was becoming a growing business, looked mild compared to what I discovered.

I was so enraged that I had allowed myself to be shut out of fully knowing our financial affairs, I was beside myself. As I privately panicked over the situation, I went into overdrive to figure out what could be done about what seemed like insurmountable debt. After months of juggling his empty properties, it seemed that life was beginning to settle down again.

During this same time, I became worried about *him*. We regularly spoke back and forth by phone or through letters, but then suddenly nothing. At first I wasn't *so* worried. It wasn't *that* unusual. But then, as my letters and calls went unanswered for weeks, and the weeks turned into months, I became frantic. When he finally did call, he told me he had been on extended night patrols and could not be contacted, but in actuality he had been enmeshed in an affair with a young woman he had met in the Philippines. She had three children of her own, and was carrying his child. Little did I know that, before returning home, he had promised to marry her.

Against this backdrop, a 'Dear John' letter came in the midst of my work day. Employees were buzzing around in the basement office where I was in the midst of a fledgling design and publishing company born out of my desire to stay home with my kids.

Just as my soul had selected, and in the midst of the world of emotional environment I was born into, I was at the end game of my self-denial cycle. The choices I had made that constantly over-rode my intuition were now getting ready to play out in the all too familiar emotions that I had been stuffing for years. Fear that had, by this time, turned into many permutations of grief, abandonment, isolation, resentment, anger and judgment were about to come up in one big wall of emotion, and was a direct match to the database I had first built as a young child.

True to form, with my soul's planting of that first vision of demise, I had been given a big clue for what was coming. It all came back to me in that moment as I read the words, "...now I know what love is."

From the first bit of knocking on doors in my newly adopted home, I had become compulsive and obsessive about building the business, in part to support the growing demands of the homefront but also to succeed at what I set out to do.

Somewhere between striving-to-survive and pushing-to-succeed, I began sensing that economic freedom was my ticket to freeing myself from that all too familiar feeling of inner turmoil. I worked at high speed from morning until night, and did not stop. My life was like a stressed-out production machine. I felt the answer to everything was to keep working harder.

The more I pushed to cover all the bases, the kids suffered my attention. The home life became stressed beyond belief. There was never enough love and attention to go around. By perpetuating the illusion of needing to be all things to all people, I lost sight of my primary goal to be fully present *for them.* My role as mom and caregiver, as life got harder, diminished both in quality and quantity.

Each day, I woke up with a mission of redirecting a life that seemed always on the edge of failure. I had worked myself into being a high-wired, lonely, sad, overworked entrepreneur, over-worried wife of an absentee partner, and single parent with no life of my own. I was not pleasing anyone else around me, and most certainly not myself.

Shortly after I received the news, I told my staff that I did not know what was going to happen, but that I would let them know as we went along. In my heart of hearts, I knew I was already tired of the fight and held onto a deep desire just to simplify my life.

Once my now estranged husband was back in the area, I was under constant attack. The one person I had trusted, at this point for almost half my life, was now my nemesis. Our children became pawns in a full-blown power struggle that took on the tones of 'black knight' type behavior to frighten me into submission. We jostled over the typical marital stuff, but when it came to pushing me to agree to separate the children and trade them between households every other year, I said no and drew the line in the sand. I filed for emergency custody and that was it; His anger turned to hatred and his actions to vindictiveness.

As I look back, the turning point in this period of 'waking up' began with the day I was in an automobile accident. When I hit another car, I totalled my little station wagon. Our daughter was injured. At the sight of seeing his sister bleeding from the mouth, James became hysterical. I was in a state of shock. The event in and of itself was traumatic enough, but because, by this time, my now estranged husband was in full-blown attack mode, I didn't want to tell him. After returning from overseas, he was back in North Carolina and constantly threatened to snatch the children from school and to take them out of state if I didn't give in to his demands.

Not long after that, late one evening, I received a call. As I listened, I heard, "thinking of filing a lawsuit against you to collect damages...I went and got a copy of the police report...suing you in her name..."

As I heard the words, my heart first dropped to my gut as it usually did, but this time, through the rush of emotion, I felt a deep eerie peace wash over me. This peace stayed with me and somehow gave me renewed strength to get on with getting on.

An aside to this part of my learning was that Spirit showed me just how protected I was. This accident happened just *one day* after I secured new automobile insurance. Earlier in the week, I panicked after receiving a notice that he had taken me off our joint policy without notifying me in advance. I quickly called another company and obtained new coverage.

With our day in court quickly approaching, and attorneys prepared to battle it out, we finally agreed to a property settlement and to respectfully go our separate ways. As my soul called for clearing, it was not meant to be. After all was said and done, I found a mistake in the deed to the farm. This sent me back to my attorney, and for months on end, the ugliness just got just got uglier.

His refusal to sign the corrected deed pushed me into a deeper state of terror than I ever thought possible. For the first time since all the turmoil hit, I began to loose hope of ever outrunning my diminishing ability to survive my circumstances.

By the time we first settled our affairs, my ability to keep up with the mounting financial obligations had already diminished, but in the midst of this new round of wrangling, it seemed that what could go wrong, did.

In the dead heat of summer, the farm's water supply stopped flowing. The old well-pump burnt up and had to be replaced. Less than a month after the repairs were completed, the new pump burnt out from mud that was clogging the system and a new well had to be dug. That winter, the old furnace that fueled the radiator system broke down and the pipes froze. The old boiler was quickly fixed, but then just days later, the oil tank that supplied the fuel to heat the house had to be replaced.

While my financial state deteriorated further from all the extra money going out the door, I waited for him to sign the deed. Without a clear deed, I could not do anything to lessen the burden. I felt the only thing to do to stay financially afloat was to work harder and to expand the business to keep it all in play. This phase of growing while under such emotional duress, was grueling and the load felt like I was operating with a two-ton weight on my back each day.

When the marital turmoil first hit, I felt betrayed and trapped by my circumstances, but with this final round of spiteful-ness, I felt my will begin to bend. As I began to cave in to his demands just to get it over with, I pushed even harder to grow a business that would eventually crumble down around me. The faster my outer world deteriorated, the harder I worked to keep it all together. As I did so, the acts of betrayal and broken trust that were playing out in my broken marriage began to take form in my business associations and friendships. The events that followed baffled the imagination and took me by surprise, but in retrospect, they were a direct reflection of just how much I had come to distrust myself.

After a series of harsh awakenings, I finally surrendered my will to the greater will of the Divine. As I set my resolve to follow the path of inner knowing, I promised myself that no matter what people would come to think of me, or choose to believe, I would listen to my inner voice above all others. That was the bottom line.

With this promise ratified in my heart, and just as I thought life would get better by my decision to put my trust in God, it was only the beginning of the physical devastation and emotional clearing that followed.

As one part of my life after another fell away, the writing on the wall became clear; that I was not going to out-smart, out-maneuver, or out-run the result of a life built on denial and self-diminishment, duality and fear.

After winding down some parts of my business, losing others, dropping yet others, I finally decided the time had come to let the rest fall away. I was exhausted and ready to let it *all* go. In a flash of insight, I contracted with an auctioneer. Suddenly, everything was up for sale...*everything*.

It was a gut wrenching decision but, somehow, it felt right. After I signed the contract, I made another round of phone calls to inform my parents, and almost as quickly cancelled the contract. My mother would later say that she just could not bear to see me lose it all that way.

Just a short time later, they became the new owners and I prepared to purchase a new home, but in the end, the once bussling basement office became my bedroom while my kids stayed upstairs. I felt the constant nag of humiliation but at peace with my path.

There are never any 'best' and 'right' decisions when you are in pain, but there is always 'highest' and 'greatest.' The distinction between these two feelings is that one way is propelled by 'should's' and 'have to's,' and the other comes from a place of peace.

The choice for me was a simple one to make, because in the moment of my decision, I felt a sense of timeless peace wash over me. However, allowing that feeling to guide me did not mean that what followed was a cake walk. When we are on the path to correct a pattern of lower vibrational learning, the correction process can sometimes seem like a living hell for awhile.

In order to protect their investment, my choice was to wait before dissolving the rest of my financial affairs. These next two years felt like a slow arduous death. It set up a whole dynamic of dialoguing, sometimes on a week-to-week basis with the very creditors who had financially backed me in times of growth. Many were not only my creditors but my friends. The sheriff became a regular visitor to my basement door.

As I worked to unravel the tangled web of my past misgivings, and continued to forge a living from the ashes of a dying enterprise, my hourly, daily focus became a matter of keeping myself away from the edge of diving deep into the emotional pit of despair and feeling such anxiety about my future.

The most painful part of this particular lesson was the falling away of friends, employees, colleagues and family members.

The reaction of those who had known me before the crash, and after was profound. Some didn't know what to say, or turned away altogether. I felt such judgment and wrath; Yet, others compassionately stepped forward. I felt that I was an outcast in the very community I had grown to love. Family members closest to the situation broadcast my fear, and theirs, out to our larger family system or turned away out of resentment and disgust.

I have since learned that a group or family holds onto the vibrations of fear to amplify and act it out in many ways. It hangs on like an old shirt waiting to be tossed.

There were many times when I would process feelings in the aftermath of an interaction or gathering or just sit in the feeling of judgment. My heart, by this time, was fully focused on the Divine, but there were times when I actually believed that God had played a dirty trick on me.

By my late-thirties, my marriage, business, homelife and standing in the community had fully disintegrated. Everything I had ever worked for had fallen away. It had been a slow painful death of the old me, and I had participated in my own funeral.

In retrospect, the harshest part of my lesson, which at the time seemed like a kind of hellish purgatory, provided me the opportunity to grieve, forgive, and to affirm my faith. It forced me to shed the labels of who I thought I was, and who I was not. During family visits, as my siblings chattered about wallpaper, travel and the minor inconveniences of life, I silently felt blessed to have a roof over my head and the love of God in my heart.

After living so far away for many years, I was afforded the opportunity to get to know my parents again. As stability and consistency returned to my children's day-to-day lives, they began to feel safe and secure.

The culmination of these experiences provided me with a perfect reflection of what I was feeling inwardly! My soul most certainly prompted me to break down the shell that separated my false sense of self from my God self. What I learned from this time in my life, is that if ever I had any doubt about how I would choose to live my life, by the time I came through the hell fire of change, I had no doubt by the time my life began transitioning into a new phase of learning.

Looking back, I went through three distinct learning phases: The first phase was to awaken from the unconscious way of making choices; the second was to surrender my will to the greater will of God; and the third was to test my resolve to maintain my focus and attention on the Divine within.

It was only after I began consciously surrendering my fears to God, and trusting my inner knowing, that whenever I would become paralyzed with fright or demoralized, the face of God would appear before me, or I'd hear a voice of reassurance.

It was only later that I came to a fuller understanding that just as our souls call out for change, God is there to provide the tools for that transformation to occur, but only when we are ready. In fact, God is never *not* there. The Source of our creation is always there, within us, prompting us to awaken to our divine nature.

In some of those darker days, I met individuals who saw through my fears to the little girl who was trying to escape her self-imposed agony. They extended their friendship and shared their wisdom. Through them, I learned to sit quietly and wait for the answers to come through the roar of my mind.

While in the midst of the most dramatic part of such inner turmoil, I was scared and confused, but I also felt the Divine fully present in my life. While I trudged through the emotional and financial ruins of the day, I was also diving deep into a spiritual transformation that took on mystical qualities that, to this day ,I do not fully understand. By allowing the Divine to permeate my being, I experienced direct communion with those who guide me. The veil of understanding was lifted and there on the other side of my limited version of reality were the angels and guides just waiting to help.

Now I can see, much more clearly, the path of resistance I chose. Even as I made many of these early choices unconsciously. I came to the understanding that my life, up to that point in time, didn't have to be so harsh. I had grown up with the feeling of being unprotected from the harshness of the world around me—a vibrational frequency I brought in with me and reinforced by the many choices I had made along the way. Through all my trials and tribulations, it never occurred to me to ask God, the *All of Everything*, to help me gain access to that inner Light I had been seeking. It wasn't until just a few years ago, that I realized the greater depth of this initial awakening. I have come to appreciate the fuller extent of Divine guidance in my life at the time.

The interesting part about this particular lesson is that it is only one aspect of the many lessons I have learned, with emphasis on the word *many*. In fact, I am still experiencing life much the same way as when I was living unconsciously—one day at a time. The difference now is that I live life solely for the sake of realizing my soul's highest expression., which is pure unadulterated joy!

It takes a choice, determination and practice, but I am here to tell you that there is an easier, more joyful way to live. Skat!! I say, just skat to fear."

About the Writings

I feel incredibly blessed to have shared many of these early learnings with a dear friend and compatriot of heart. We would sit in the quiet of the moment and ask that God open our hearts. What followed was a series of energetically delivered teachings that can only be fully appreciated in hindsight.

As I became more comfortable with the process of being transfigured by Spirit, I started asking questions. This manifested as either holding a question in thought as my Guides spoke or asking a question once I felt the energy of their teaching come to close. The lessons I received in this manner pushed me to surrender my fears and to see things differently. It taught me to trust my heart rather than rely so much on the strength of the mind. In fact, I quickly learned that in times of pain and anguish that it was always the mind (my ego) that got in the way and tripped me up. Because of a doubting mind, I held back, recoiled in indecision or allowed my Light to be suppressed by another— not exactly an enjoyable way to live.

The learning was profound even then, but over the years the knowledge I have carried with me continues to enrich my life enormously. During each session, Spirit was forever prompting me to continue on the path of right action and to tread lightly on the path to realize peace.

If you are feeling fearful in some manner, the writings following each chapter may serve to calm the nerves, the way it did for me, and put your learning into perspective.

NOTE: In some of the Writings, where necessary, the use of italics are used to separate my voice from the Guides.

MY NAME IS GOD

I am your Father. I am your Mother. All things come
from me. Everything is motivated and moved by me.

If I wish something to be done nothing can stop it.
My will is love. I will you to love your fellow man, to love
yourself, to love your God with all your heart.

I am to be on your mind and lips at all times.
Everything you do or say is to be motivated by the
divine power of God.

It is time for a separation to occur. There is no longer
any need to hate or cause for discontent within your
self and your fellow human beings. Fear is outmoded
and it is now time to step into your birthright. If you
learn to live in the spirit of my love all else will follow.

If you follow my Light and become one with it, there will
be no need for want. All the material gain in the world
does not match up with one candle from my flame. My
flame burns brightly for you.

I AM all there is. You must simply recognize me for who
I am. For I am you. We are one. We are all one,
interconnected and linked together as brothers.

We come from the same Light.
We are the same.

So rejoice in your daily existence.
Know that I am with you all times,
that you are loved.

—October 27, 1990
Sri Sathya Sai Baba

Fear is that little darkroom
where negatives are developed.

—Michael Pritchard

CHAPTER TWO

THE SOURCE OF FEAR IN OUR DIVINE NATURE

*The emotion of fear is mankind's
primal scream to the Divine within,
"Come save me from this hell!"*

Fear is a state of being

If you stop to think about it, the emotion of fear comes in all shapes and forms. It plagues the mind and makes the heart seem heavy with burden and anxiety. This state of being can be present daily, hourly or even moment to moment.

In the recesses of our mind, this assault on our peace of mind can turn quickly to terror or prolonged worry which takes its toll on the physical body. Fear can also coax us into retreat from the daily engagement in life or bring about a sense of defeat or hopelessness. I know this sounds very dramatic but in the deeper levels of our psyche, fear operates this way. When our emotions get the better of us, we may feel as though our very life is at stake with no hope of ever seeing our way out of the darkness into the light of day.

Survival, or the fear for survival, is what rules our human nature, so much so, that many have forgotten its origins. We are in fact divine beings of Light who transcend all time and space, but with every passing day we have become so enamored with the physical world that we have succumbed to our emotions. We are not the body and we are not to be fooled by fear. We are powerful creators who are in command of our lives. We may have forgotten who we are and have allowed fear to cloud our very existence, but we can be awakened from our slumber.

Among the myriad of emotions that come to the surface there are six that weigh heavy on the outcome of the human condition; they are poverty, criticism, ill health, lost love, old age, and death.

These fears are first created as a thought, then as an emotion, but it is nothing more than a state of mind which is subject to command and direction. However, we begin to project our feelings into the world and manifest them into their physical equivalent.

By learning to understand the nature of how you create your reality, you can change your thought impulses and change your beliefs. If you are a student of science, you may agree with scientists who postulate that the observer changes that which he observes through his intention, conscious or subconscious, operating within the body and mind of the observer. This is a basic theory of quantum mechanics which theorizes the dynamics of electrons, protons and other fundamental particles but it has come as a surprise to many researchers that it also holds sway over larger systems.

If you are a student of spirituality, you may have come to learn that some traditions say, "When two or more gather in my name I am there." We are so powerful that we are able to change our world by mere observation, prayer and focused intention. Learning to rely on the wisdom within you and all around you to guide your life is in proportion to the trust you place in this wisdom.

Fear manifests in the many roles we play such as parent, child, brother, sister, aunt, uncle, grandparent, romantic partner, friend, co-worker and the biggest one, our self. Our list of roles only grows longer as we progress through life. In emotional terms fear translates into our physical reality as doubt, regret, remorse, indecisiveness, confusion, discontent, worry, depression, resentment, jealously, power, lust, greed, control, malice, hate, violence.

Fear paralyzes our ability to reason, stifles the imagination, sabotages self-reliance, undermines enthusiasm, discourages initiative, leads to uncertainty, encourages procrastination and makes self-control an impossibility. It flattens one's personality, destroys critical thinking and dulls the senses. It also destroys the will power, fogs the memory and pushes failure at every turn. It dampens love and deadens the more subtle emotions of the heart, discourages friendship and invites conflicts in relationship. It leads to sleeplessness, misery and unhappiness. Despite any disillusionment with love, fear blocks our way from realizing our divine nature.

The frequency and intensity of acting out of fear is such a part of our everyday living that it may seem quite normal. Some would even venture to say that without this basic response to life, the human race would cease to survive.

At minimum, fear is a belief in scarcity and is rooted in believing that you are not capable of garnering the life you deserve, and are not good enough to achieve what you desire. These beliefs control how you react to the world around you. These are thought patterns that take form in the physical, born of the choices you have made. A sampling of these outcomes might be choosing to live in less than desirable conditions, getting less than what you deserve, thinking negatively about yourself and others, or selling yourself short.

An example of living out the belief of scarcity is the prospect of losing your job. Your mind will say, "If I lose my job I will have no place to live, no food to put on the table, no money to pay bills."

This is fear-based thinking and emoting and is how many people think. Most of us were raised to operate this way. It motivates and drives us to go deeper into the feeling of *lack*. Other examples of fear go like this: "If I do not go to school I will not get a proper education then I will not be able to get a good job."

Fear.

"If I do not work 14-16 hour days, I will not get ahead as I should and measure up."

Fear.

"If I do not act or say all the right things, dress a certain way or become a certain outside appearance by weight, size, style and manner of speaking then I will not be accepted and loved by the people I care about."

Fear.

"If I do not meet society's expectations of not achieving a certain status in life, I will be judged a failure."

Fear.

When we say and do things out of insecurity or for the sake of seeking outside approval, fear is rearing its ugly head in victory. Now, I'm not saying that going to school, getting a good job and being loved by those around you is not the way to go. What I am saying is that your motivation to do, to see and to be can be chosen differently. You can chose love over fear as your belief of choice. This is evolution. There are many examples that can be found in the Bible and many writings that reflect the teachings of Jesus of the Nazarene. He was a deeply compassionate man who anticipated his life mission long before his passing, but understood his impending death sentence just hours prior to its unfolding. He gave his life so that others could know the truth of God. This is the supreme act of choosing love over fear as he was totally aligned with the Father.

Identifying with the body and not Spirit is the root cause of all worldly suffering.

Knowing that only you are in command of your life, you may wish to ask the question of yourself, "How can I withstand the unforeseen blows that come my way if I cannot endure the reactions to my own emotions?"

Our beliefs shape our life. One example is expectation which takes the form of being concerned about doing the right thing and living up to whatever demands you may hold for yourself and those that you perceive from others. Living in a society that prides itself on the work ethic and the American way of getting ahead comes with its own brand of expectation. Each day you may work hard only to ask yourself at day's end, "Have I worked hard enough, smart enough, good enough. Did I measure up? How did I do compared to what others are doing?" On and on the dialog goes, running in the back of your mind.

Competition is another reaction that has its roots in fear. This one is ingrained in our cultural upbringing—the destructive kind of competition of needing to be thought of as better than the other person, or putting ourselves above the rest.

If your emotions are not curbed and transformed to love, fear will eventually turn to hate or violence. Violence against another is the focal point of the national and regional news media but it is nothing compared to the malice of the thoughts and words that we internalize each hour of every day.

This kind of internal violence takes form as self-degradation and self-chastisement. As an action taken against the self, it speaks volumes about buying into the belief of not measuring up. Violence against the self kills the spirit of self-love.

Even your expression of love can take form as just another form of degradation. This happens when you feel guilty or obligated to express the love you desire for yourself. It is as if your soul is calling you to freely express your emotions but you hold yourself back. Your belief in fear creates a feeling of being less than loved so that even a true expression of love will be denied or eliminated.

Fear camouflaged as love is a part of the social and cultural fabric of our society. Fear takes root every day in the actions of people who repeatedly react to life instead of acting from a balanced center. At humankind's worst, fear physically manifests as war, gangs, or spreads in waves of mass hysteria, mobs, looting and riots.

Human nature loves fear. Fear can be exciting but it can also be immobilizing in the face of threat. Fear plays out the hunter and the hunted, in a sick kind of way, as we replay the act of aggression and condemnation over and over again in our mind.

How often do you do this after having said or thought feelings of ill will toward another or felt these same hurtful feelings from someone else? The replay button may get played so many times that it becomes a part of you. Once it does, you may begin to scheme about how to get paybacks or move deeper into a feeling of being a victim of someone else's ill will. This very simplistic act of violence is repeated throughout life.

If you begin to monitor your thoughts for just a few moments you will witness many acts of malcontent and unkindness passing through the halls of your mind. All oppressive, aggressive acts stem from this primal emotion.

This feeling of always being on the edge of dissatisfaction is actually an act of self-condemnation and holds us in a kind of ego-survival mentality. By doing so we are expending inordinate amounts of energy focusing our attention on gaining the approval of others, which only perpetuates the downward spiral of self-loathing. On the outer exterior you may portray calm and peace to others, but just below the surface you are feeling fear and anxiety on every level. In traditional terms our personality traits have even been given a designation by type indicating just how intensely the outward motivators of the world drive us further into a state of fear.

Once you learn that you have bought into an external system of gaining validation of self from others, which manifests as stress, you can begin to stop it. Killer stress has a tendency to permeate every facet of our being. As a threat to your safety it triggers a primal physical response from the body. From deep within the brain, a chemical signal speeds stress hormones through the bloodstream, priming the body to be alert and ready to escape danger. When the stressful situation ends, hormonal signals switch off, but in our modern society, many hold onto anxiety and worry about daily events and relationships. Adrenaline continues to wash through the system in high levels, never leaving the blood and tissues.

This played out in my own life, when after years of obsessing over the ashes of a life I had left behind and rebuilding another, my body started to break down. I didn't recognize the symptoms until very recently when I began noticing a tremendous energy drain, short-term memory loss and lack of motivation. After finding a doctor who practiced holistic medicine, I discovered I was suffering from stage three adrenal exhaustion, a direct result of sustaining high levels of stress over the years.

The leading source of stress for adults is their jobs but this underlying fear has also escalated in children, teenagers, college students and the elderly for other reasons, including: increased crime, violence and other threats to personal safety; unyielding peer pressures that lead to substance abuse and other unhealthy lifestyle habits; social isolation and loneliness; the erosion of family ties and spiritual values; and the loss of other strong sources of social support.

Fear is so integrated into the human experience that even if you have transcended many of your misperceptions, you are bound to experience the lower emotions at some point in your life. Fear may motivate and drive your actions, but it is only a state of being. The core essence of who you are is love, and love experienced as the Divine will open your heart to another way of living.

When I was feeling so consumed with the effects of crushing stress, the only thing that gave me temporary relief was running. I'd get up in the early morning and run while the children slept, then would come back to feed the animals, get the children ready for school and start my work day. But that was a temporary fix. Nothing else seemed to give me permanent relief. I have since come to rely on Spirit to show me the way. Learning to first acknowledge how I am feeling, then to trust in a higher power of that which created me is the key that always allows peace of mind to be restored.

How to recognize and overcome
the misconceptions of fear

How can you identify fear-based beliefs? You may think that you must make a commitment, meet a schedule or perform a service because we live in a world that demands that we surrender our inner Light. In actuality many of us move through our world as though we are unworthy of realizing our freedom from living merely to survive. This action, motivated by our belief, is an act of fear.

Fear taking form as a belief about who we are and who are we not is the craziest convoluted mess humankind has bought into yet.

In popular culture, love is a cliché of sorts. It is over amplified and over simplified in many respects. We may know a lot about fear because we get heavy doses of it every day, but love is more elusive.

Many of us feel very comfortable expressing fear but feel like a 'fish out of water' when our hearts begin to open. As a society, I think it is a fair statement that many feel they do not get enough love in life.

All these outward signs of fear signal a lack of love. Love moves and drives all inner emotions to a place of peace and contentment. When you are in that space of inner calm, there is no need to experience struggle. This includes how you perceive the world as you move through your day. Check your reactions to the people and situations you encounter against what you are feeling inwardly. Do the two feelings match? If not, ask yourself, "why not?"

The ultimate goal is for our inner and outer worlds to come into alignment with the vibration of love. This was the teaching and the path of Jesus and other masters who came to show humanity the way. He demonstrated that the way to realizing one's freedom, on every plane of existence was to transform the self into the highest expression of love. Jesus once told his disciples that they shall not want, for they have everything in the Father. Throughout his life he taught that we are to love God with all our hearts. Only then will we see our way into heaven. This heaven is not described as something that is *out there* somewhere. Heaven is within our very being. It is a vibrational frequency that can only be attained by merging with the Divine. His life taught us this.

TAKE THE FEAR CHECKLIST

If you'd like to get a reading on where you are in the continuum of experiencing fear over love, here's a quick checklist. Before you proceed, take a moment to get quiet. With each relationship focus on how you are feeling. Focus on the first spike of emotion that comes up before you have a chance to allow your mind to think further into the person. What comes up when you think of:

- your boss/business partner?
- your mother?
- your father?
- sister?
- brother?
- child?
- best friend from the third grade?
- your first boyfriend/girlfriend?
- your wife/husband/life partner right now?
- your dog/cat/parakeet/most beloved pet?
- you?

I encourage you to write them down. Write down the first word that comes to mind for each on a separate piece of paper and keep it safe. After reading this book and applying the techniques, refer back to that list and see if you notice a change.

These are just a few for starters. If you find that you have mixed emotions about any of the above listed relationships then you are influenced, driven or motivated by fear on some level. As you focus on each relationship, if you feel an inner peace and joy, then you are well on your way to living in the vibration of joy.

Fear is a lower vibration of existence while love is experienced in the absence of, and sometimes in spite of, fear. We can feel the heaviness of fear in our bodies, but we are more than the body-mind connection. We are dynamic beings of energy and whatever we think and feel emits out into the world as a vibrational frequency.

The human body is not just the physical body. It is easy to understand the significance of this dense part of ourselves because we can see it. The body is also comprised of an auric field that contains multiple fields of energy. This human energy field is comprised of electro-magnetic waves of vibrational frequencies that reflect the subtle life energies within the body and can tell us much about our health, character, mental activity and emotional state. It shows disease often long before the onset of symptoms.

These multiple layers of energy bodies can be likened to the effect of static electricity when we rub our feet along a carpet or a balloon on our head. Few of us can see these energies but we can feel it. Our auric field is egg shaped and energetically holds our mental, emotional and spiritual states of well being.

The expressions of 'feeling it in the gut' or 'having a lump in the throat,' or 'heartache' are mental reminders for what is occurring energetically. With every thought, feeling and emotion our energy fields will intensify or weaken and our auric field will change size, shape and color accordingly.

With the work I am called to do with groups and individuals, I can see their fields change as they incorporate the higher vibrations of thought into their light bodies. There are energetic streams of light-wave frequencies that link us to others. If you become sensitized to the understanding that whatever you do, feel or think affects another, then you will better see what changes you are being called to make in your own life. Your soul gives you a very big clue as to how you are feeling about yourself by how you perceive others.

If you will just take a moment and think of someone who really irritates you, or someone you feel is less than who he or she should be, I will prove my point. What you are feeling in this moment is a direct reflection of a feeling you are holding onto about yourself. You may not recognize this quality within you, but this person would not irritate you if this vibration were not a part of you. The stronger the emotion, the stronger the vibration within you.

We all have a tendency to project our fears onto others, but knowing this, you can now use it as a tool to cut the many energetic cords that bring you pain and hardship.

This is not just my own knowing. Studies and experiments have proven the power of feelings and have developed technology to measure electro-magnetic fields within us. During the past 25 years over 500 scientific studies have been conducted on the subject of how positive thought can change our surroundings. Of these studies, Transcendental Meditation (TM) alone showed the wide-ranging benefits for all aspects of life. Forty-two of these studies have shown that when one percent of the population of any town or country practices meditation, or when the square root of one percent of a population practice, there are dramatic positive improvements in the entire society. One city experienced a temporary drop in criminal activity.

Researchers have also developed mechanical instruments to capture and measure human energy readings. One that is used in hospitals the world over is called the MRI, or magnetic resonance imaging. When protons are placed in a magnetic field, they become capable of receiving and then transmitting electro-magnetic energy. The strength of the transmitted energy is proportional to the number of protons in the tissue. Signal strength is modified by properties of each proton's micro-environment, such as its mobility and the local homogeneity of the magnetic field.

The use of vibrational frequencies have even made it to the shelf of the consumer through products such as a small battery powered device that repels mosquitoes by sending out a specific sound-wave frequency.

It was early pioneers like Sir Isaac Newton who merged Greek philosophy and Judeo-Islamic-Christian principles in pursuit of unraveling the mysteries of the universe. What we now call the laws of physics, early scientists regarded as God's abstract creation science. In modern times, we take it for granted that the physical world is ordered and intelligible. Now, we are once again called to open our minds to explore our universe in new ways. As we shift our thinking away from the reality of living in a world of physicality to one that is comprised of energy and light wave frequencies, what and how we consciously create must also change.

As you compare differences in feeling between the vibrations of fear and love, liken them to two rivers. One way of being is fast and rushing; the other calm, still, flowing. Fear is a rapid, treacherous flow while love is smooth, joyous and gently allowing. Fear causes for alarm and discontent, but love quiets the mind and calms the heart. When immersed in the river of love, there is a pureness of Light that is indescribable.

The simple forms of fear are overt. There is no mistaking these feelings. They can hit you over the head everyday in very dramatic or such subtle and not so subtle ways. You may feel fear as a knot in your stomach, or as tension and stress. Many disassociate this feeling from their actions, which take form as boredom, anger, resentment or violence. The ways we manifest fear are endless.

Love on the other hand is not a pushing, nagging sort of sensation. It is soft and subtle but can also burst forth with fervency that quickly calms the vibration of fear. As you learn to discern the difference between these two feelings, you will begin to loosen the grip of fear.

How do you transcend a fear-driven state of mind? Do you want to? Fear as a state of mind that may drive you to succeed in worldly terms, but this way of living does not ensure outward success. Your belief that it does perpetuates this way of being.

You may say, "Yes, I'm tired of allowing fear to shape my life," but in this 'yes' there is a doubt. This doubt drives your very fear of fear itself. To change from living in a state of fear to one that puts you on the path to freedom requires courage to face the unknown. It takes courage to transcend the lower vibrations of fear. These feelings of doubt, indecision, discontent, worry, greed, hate, and violence are so woven into the fabric of our society that it is difficult to gain a perspective on just how steeped you may be in it. Precious few have been shown the way out of fear, as a state of being, without experiencing doubt along the way.

Doubt is often the stumbling block that continues to plague our final release of fear because it is a mirror to the mind's imagination. With courage you can realize your freedom by releasing the beliefs that hold you to your current pattern of pain and hardship. This requires an act of faith that can only happen by leaping into your own void of understanding and will, at times, challenge the very fiber of your being. This kind of leap is accomplished by learning to trust your intuition and will prompt you again and again to follow your inner guidance.

The first step to overcoming the perpetual state of fear-based living is by making the heartfelt decision to do so. After that, you will be challenged to let go of the beliefs that hold you to your current pattern of living and to embrace the feelings of peace, joy and love. By making the choice to change and implementing the tools and strategies outlined in the following chapters, you will begin to more fully identify with your heart's desire.

Just say, "yes" to freedom, and the real you will step forward as you say goodbye to fear.

"Skat!!" I say, "just *skat* to fear."

LETTING GO OF FEAR

Guide: Blessed be the souls of Light and love, of harmony and fate. For you see my dear child it is faith which brings all humankind together. It is always the fate, the destiny, the vision of God which brings you to me.

It is always the burning desire to understand wisdom itself. You are the Light which lights the way. You are the child within the universe.

You are one with God and all its creation. Do not let the forces of darkness overtake your peace.

Let there always be a peace, a sweetness to your fate.

Allow Light to surround you, to protect you. Do allow. Do allow the fairies, the helpers, the doers, the forces of nature to help you maintain balance from within.

I will always be with you. Do not fear. It is with great regret that I cannot reveal myself to you fully at this present time.

Do not fear.

Be always in the Light, of the Light and to merge with the divine presence always.

Do not forsake me. I will always be with you.

— June 4, 1993
Sri Sathya Sai Baba

RELEASING WORRY

I cannot explain why I doubt, cry and whine about my world. I do not understand my doubt when I have been shown I have nothing to fear, but fear I do.

Guides: Worry is a lack of faith in God. You must give up worry if you are to know God. Roadblocks come in many forms and the biggest is the denial of love itself. You must be disciplined, have courage and remain of humble spirit if you are to know God. This knowing will not be realized by boasting or judging another.

You are alive to learn that you are God incarnate in physicality. Some come kicking and screaming to unite with the Divine; others come slowly, swimmingly, smoothly. The act of surrender begins with a progression of thought then a leap.

Some get thrust into the fire of understanding while others refuse to accept that there is a God. It is the acceptance that is most difficult. One is rooted in the physical. The other is invisible but just as tangible. Humankind uses these proprieties and feelings to simulate the language of the heart, but there is no substitute. Without uniting one's heart with the Divine you will find no peace.

Once you have discovered and acknowledged the difference between these two ways of operating in the world, there is no turning back. Progressing into the heart center of God is your primary requirement for change. It is the change of heart that will eventually bring you peace.

Following your intuition breaks the deadlock of the mind and brings with it a deeper understanding of the heart.

All of Creation is standing on Tiptoe
Waiting to see the sons and daughters
of God come into their fullness.

—Unknown

CHAPTER THREE

WHAT TO DO WHEN FEAR OVERTAKES YOU

Our creations take form then we step back
in our doubt and question what is happening
in our world—we are afraid.

Tools for Overcoming Fear

A friend most recently said, "fake it 'til you make it." He was referring to that feeling of peace and inner happiness that at times is so fleeting it lasts only for a day, a week, or for just a few moments.

When living life in a perpetual state of fright you may often find yourself immersed in some crisis or form of terror that is bound to creep into your consciousness and disturb your peace of mind. When your peace is disturbed you are actually surrendering your very life force to something less than who you are.

Who knows the reason why the deep roots and learned traits of fear are triggered within us. When our emotions get churned up, our world can quickly turn into chaos as we react in anger or recoil in abject terror. When we feel threatened, our peace of mind and sense of safety and wellbeing feels compromised. These states of being are feelings that may also trigger deeper more ingrained fear-based beliefs.

67

When you are in a state of agitation or disassociation, it is likely that panic will overtake you. Once your emotional defenses are exhausted, a feeling of helplessness can easily find its way into your inner sanctum. When this happens you are misidentifying with the very source of your creation so completely that you are giving your power away. This occurs because you are unconsciously relinquishing your responsibility as a spiritual being to others.

The final stage of becoming overwhelmed by inner turmoil is descending into the downward spiral of hopelessness. If this begins to occur, you may think that there is no way out and you just may decide to give up on life altogether. A classic example of hopelessness can be found in the poverty of the world's ghetto populations. Deplorable living conditions are a physical manifestation of humanity giving up on the self. Some may decide to stop taking care of life's most basic needs or abuse their bodies by not heeding the early warning signs of ill health. Then again, some may actively surrender their life force altogether and commit suicide.

Fully immersed in these depressed states of being, you will find it very difficult to discern what direction or action is needed to maneuver your way out of such oppressive feelings of fear, let alone make the best choice for yourself.

However the *first step* to overcoming fear is to learn to quiet the mind and open your heart. Quieting the mind is a way of accessing the inner recesses of your heart. If you are busy thinking, strategizing, worrying, then you cannot possibly be relaxed enough to allow Spirit to flow through you. When the mind shuts down, the heart will naturally open. It may feel like a yearning at first. That is O.K. Yearning is a start if it is a feeling of wanting to know God—not the pleading, begging sort of emoting we are known to do in times of trouble.

Peace of mind can be restored even in the most challenging of circumstances. If God can 'move mountains over rivers' then you, with a heartfelt willingness to surrender to the better part of who you are, can calm your emotions and clear your mind.

I have come to understand that fear is often used as a push for learning, which serves as a very valuable motivator. You can learn to use it as a tool for this purpose or feel that you are the victim of your circumstances. Either way it is a choice to see the world as *stuff happening to you*, or to embrace life in all its possibilities.

Life's hardest lessons don't have to be unpleasant but when you feel forced to make decisions in panic, fear may give you that extra push to begin taking responsibility for your creation, or you will wallow in it until you do. There are times when you are in such a state of confusion that it can actually feel like your very life force is being sucked right out. This is experienced as an extreme energy drain accompanied by a total lack of ability to think clearly.

Either way you choose to learn, your soul calls out for transformation. Dawn breaks anew when you begin taking charge of your life for the better. The *second step* to making this happen is to make the choice for love. When you finally come to this point in your life cycle, it is because you have fully recognized that living in fear just has to go. As you emerge from this often-painful part of your awakening, the *third step* is to surrender your fears to God, and with this surrender comes a deep peace. It is the kind of feeling that quiets the mind and centers your heart on an often times profound sense of gratitude for all that you have been through. Without those experiences you would not have come to this point in your self-discovery process. For me, this feeling of just having come through the eye of stormy emotions is always humbling and personally revealing.

So why do so many of us choose to learn the hard way? Some may say that life just happens and we have to roll with the punches. Others decide that fighting is the best way to overcome life's obstacles. Both of these approaches to life are fatalistic in nature and rely on fate.

You may look at your circumstances in this baneful fashion by reacting to life in self-pity or by latching onto someone else to solve your problems. By doing so, you will continue to recreate the very same set of circumstances that led you down the path of discontent and unhappiness over and over and over again. The alternate reaction is to take charge of your life by reclaiming your power as a spiritual being of Light.

Newton's third law of motion states, "For every action there is a reaction." The spiritual law of cause and effect works this way and is our higher self's way of teaching by turning up the heat and repeating the performance under new, but surprisingly similar circumstances. It is the way we learn. Why? Because spiritual beings choose to learn this way. When a child plays, life is grand. When it's time to learn something new and the child does not listen to his father, the child may fall and skin his knee. In his pain, the child stops and cries for help. The father comes and helps then teaches the child how to play more wisely. Once the child realizes that all he has to do is ask for help and his father will teach him new and useful things, he evolves from a stubborn child to a conscious participant in life.

Another example of this concept is a woman who falls in love with the same type of person over and over again until finally after yet another break up, she decides to look within. She realizes after much inner searching that she has recreated the same deep emotional wound that first pushed her to unconsciously deny the love of another as a way to protect her heart from further pain and suffering. Once she clears this emotion from her psyche, she will no longer attract the same situation to herself.

God uses fear to push us to learn. We are not the mind-body continuum. We are the Divine incarnate in physicality.

The Spiritual Guides say that we are here to learn how to love and the time continuum has only been set up so that we will feel the need to push ourselves more deeply into our lessons. The illusion of time promotes a sense of continuity and pressure to get it right. If we understand our true nature as spiritual beings then we will understand that our ultimate goal is to learn to love our self and all of humanity unconditionally. We are to remain humble as we work to transcend our self-imposed limitations. As we learn this basic lesson of giving and receiving love, we will no longer need to repeat our lessons over and over again.

Just remember that you are a spiritual being who is doing the choosing. You can learn the easy way or the hard way and there is no judgment in whichever way you pick. God does not judge your method of learning. It is merely a matter of choice. With each thought and intent, you are making the choice of how you will learn. Now that you realize choices can be made easy by listening to your inner voice or hard by your ego-driven motives, pay attention to any signs of discomfort and decipher what they mean to you and the path you are on.

Fear is a good alarm system for steering us away from getting off track. Once you begin feeling discomfort, you can get yourself re-centered by quieting your mind and discerning what is before you. Then you can set your intent for transcending the difficulty while asking that Spirit lead the way.

There are times when you may sense that you are back-sliding into turmoil and hardship. Stop and realize that you are experiencing these difficult feelings but to a lesser degree. Once you realize what lesson your soul is trying to help you through, you can then release the belief that is causing the fear.

You may wish to hold onto the old at all costs because of the emotional comfort familiarity brings. Yes, this may sound strange but fear is comfortable for most because it is the only thing we have ever known. It keeps us in a position of feeling needed, as a part of our families and social systems because we feel we are part of a shared experience. Much of our world is structured in a way that glorifies, supports and encourages pain.

Have you ever heard the term 'misery loves company?' You may be like many who find it easier to live in misery than embrace the unknown, even when it is literally killing you. The trepidation the unknown brings may pale to the comfort of misery. At least you know how miserable you are, and you feel safe in a convoluted yet predictable kind of way.

Maybe you are reading this book because you have grown tired of living that same old broken record over and over again and have decided something just has to go. When this occurs, the inner voice may sound something like this: "I've had enough of being tired, scared, broke, sick, unhappy, bored, depressed, unloved..." On the conscious level, you have acknowledged that you are ready for change. Does your subconscious agree?

The path to finding peace of mind in the midst of chaos is often times a rocky one, but well worth the effort. In the following passages, I have outlined some of the basic strategies that I have discovered for breaking through the mind-body connections that are cause for so much pain and confusion. You may wish to use this as a guide but keep an open mind. Take what works for you and leave the rest behind.

Before you begin, I have just one bit of advice. I can't stress this enough. Be kind; Be patient with yourself and know that when you are trying on new concepts for transcending fear, you are bound to revert back to your old patterns and behaviors. That's OK. For every relapse there is a new awakening just around the corner.

As you are going through your most difficult learning, stick with it and know that the heavy emotions that are bound to come up will pass through your mind. The release process can be likened to the peeling of an onion—one layer at a time. Each time you feel you have backslid into the belief of fear, just remember that you are releasing the layers of lower emotions one by one, and know that *this too shall pass.*

Tools for Overcoming Fear

1. Witness your emotions.

When fear strikes, at some level, you may become aware that a deeper part of yourself is truly in charge. The personality self (the part of you that experiences spur of the moment reactions) has been known to cause much grief and insecurity in the way it reacts to situations and events. Therein lies a deeper part of you that, however faint in times of turmoil, knows there is another way of living at hand.

When you find yourself in a state of confusion, it is helpful to stop for a moment and witness your emotions. Rather than projecting your focus outwardly and getting swept away with the enormity of what you are facing, learn to witness what you are thinking and feeling. This is the beginning of learning to separate yourself from the lower reactive part of your personality self.

No matter what is going on around you, just remember that everything you are feeling *is about you*. One example of this concept is when two people are sitting together watching a movie. One may feel uplifted while the other becomes deeply disturbed by what they are watching. It's the same in life, how we perceive and what we discern from our personal experiences is determined by how we react to them. When we are happy it is because we have chosen to experience life in a proactive manner. Another good example of this concept is to imagine that you are at a county fair walking through the funhouse and enter a hall of mirrors. Which reflection do you choose to look at? The one that makes you happy, sad, mad or glad? You choose the picture.

As you learn to keep your focus within, you will begin to ask yourself such questions as, "What am I feeling now?" and "What is this emotion I am feeling trying to teach me?" Larger life questions such as "What do I want?" and "What will make me happy? " can also be asked but only if you are willing to keep the focus of your answers on what you are feeling.

As you begin recognizing the patterns and behaviors of your actions as being mere reflections of what you are learning, then you have effectively shifted your viewpoint inward.

As mentioned in chapter one, as I was working to shore up the ashes of my marriage, I had not yet learned trust my intuition. In my personal and professional life I was still relying on other people to tell me what they thought I should do about matters that only I could decide. One major awakening was the linchpin that pushed me into a major personal crisis and my business into a financial tailspin.

I worked closely with a very bright, capable, dedicated woman. This was a person I trusted with my life. She was an emotional support for me when I was going through the very harshest part of my marriage breakup. We had been working together for several years. I considered her one of my closest friends and right arm when it came to managing the advertising sales staff, and selling for one very large contract.

As we expanded the business, I began coming out of my personal crisis but ignored the signs of stress in her as she quietly suffered the loss of her mother. We were so used to working together that when she said a task was complete, I trusted just that.

On one such project, her job was to secure advertising contracts for a very large publication. As the deadline got closer and closer, my repeated inquiries as to her progress were met with an 'everything is fine' kind of reply. My intuition told me otherwise. I knew something was wrong but with all the other demands on my time and our history together, I did not follow-up and get firm enough with my requests to be informed.

By the time I decided something was just not right altogether, and directly challenged her, we were on the brink of a deadline with no room for an extension. We closed the project and my company took an enormous loss. This was not the worst part. I sustained such a huge financial blow that it pushed my business into a financial tailspin. Not only was I devastated by the circumstances, I was forced to begin downsizing and dismantling a business I had grown to love. My staff had long become my extended family, but by the time the pieces began to crumble, many had already begun to turn away in resentment or disgust. In the midst of pain and anguish, I realized I was about to get the very thing I had first longed for—to release and simplify—but now it would be a harder more anguish-ridden fall.

If Spirit wanted to send me a message about listening to my inner voice, I finally got it. By the time the revelation for what was coming hit home, I found myself retreating to the third floor conference room. As I look back, it must have been a sight to see as one of my staff members found me crouched on the floor in the fetal position crying like a baby. My life, at that time was chock full of metaphors for what was coming, but I was so busy running away from everything I feared, I just was not getting it.

This single event accompanied a successive string of undoings on the home front, set off a deep period of introspection and inquiry into another part of myself that I perceived as broken. I just could not understand what it was. As I worked to step back and witness my emotions, I learned to clear a long ingrained pattern of trusting when I should question—ignoring my inner voice when I needed to listen.

As I dug deeper into this dynamic and learned to witness the emotions I was feeling, I discovered that my view of the world was still steeped in victim consciousness. No doubt I had bought into the belief of being a victim and had projected this belief out into the world. When I finally got it, that I had created my own misery, I affirmed my worthiness and devoted more time to breaking the old pattern. My soul's intent was to get me to trust, so what better way than to send me into such a tailspin to finally get it!

Once I began to consistently witness my emotions, I began to more fully understand the many patterns of self-denial. With this new found wisdom, I vowed to listen to my intuition and honor my inner voice above the roar of the outside world, but there was a deeper learning to come.

The path to personal empowerment is accomplished by taking total responsibility for what we are thinking, feeling and doing in our world. As you take command of your life, you will begin to unlock the doors of learning that have been hidden up until now.

You are the lead actor in your own play. Therefore, it is wise that you discern what you are feeling and thinking before you decide to take action. On the personality level, you may not choose how others interact with you, but on the soul level you create every day-to-day experience for the sake of learning.

Even as we witness our thoughts and actions this way, the emotions do have a way of getting the better of us. When you find that you are overwhelmed by life and are reacting to an incident or situation out of fear, stop; get quiet and listen to what you are feeling. Go into witness mode for just a moment. This is a simple act of regrouping and taking a step back to see what you have created before deciding to take action. This brief witnessing period serves three purposes:

1. It provides you the time needed to regroup and to

remember who you are;

2. allows you to take a second look at how you are to align yourself with your highest good, and;

3. ensures a sacred space to decide what and how you will act, or if you will take the lesser option by reacting to what is in front of you.

I'm not advising you to be self-absorbed or self-calculating. Life can certainly be most pleasurable and delightful when you are immersed in your learning, but when you are confronted with difficult feelings or situations, it is important to pause and remember who you are.

As you begin to acquaint yourself with this way of moving through your day, you will notice, as you witness your thoughts and feelings, the many strings of attachments that bind you to fear. Anyone who remembers past slights or regrets with detail, or recounts every nuance of how they have been hurt is fearful of self-accountability.

Have you ever heard the phrase, 'carrying your old baggage around?' I have learned with the gift of inner sight that this is a literal statement. Until or unless this lower energy is transmuted into higher vibrational frequencies you cannot lighten your load.

If a memory causes you pain and hardship, then it is calling out to be cleared from your auric field. As you move through life, every thought, feeling or emotion you have ever had is stored in your energy bodies. If you do not transmute these thought patterns to a higher vibration they may take form as a feeling of emotional heaviness. If left unattended these energy forms calcify and turn into mental, emotional and physical illnesses.

Now, when I find that an old memory or situation keeps popping up, this is a sure signal that I'm being called to release something that is no longer serving me. I especially pay attention to my emotions. Feelings guide us to our soul's awakening but are also a way to discern our wellness. When our inner self is ready to heal some fragmented part of our being, we call up a memory that brings forth a belief that is rooted in fear. These promptings can be subtle, or not so subtle.

Your higher self speaks to you by providing you with experiences that can sometimes bring a wave of physical or mental challenges into your life or by presenting a person or situation that is less than pleasurable. I call this mirroring the change you desire. Since you are the creator of your world, everything in it is for your learning. When confronted with a situation or memory that brings you anything less than joy, learn to ask the following questions:

What am I feeling?

What belief is no longer serving me?

What am I to release?

What have I learned from this?

Is there a pattern here and if so what does it reveal?

2. Quiet the mind.

If you are like me in times of stress, your mind races as the emotions run wild. As hard as it may seem to become quiet when you are all churned up, this is exactly what must be done. Set aside a specific part of your day, even if you do so for only a few minutes. Find a quiet place away from the television, radio and any other distractions that may interfere with this process.

Whatever time you pick, all noise and distractions must stop to allow you to sit quietly for a few moments each day. Sit and listen in the stillness of the moment to clear your mind of all thought.

At first it may seem utterly ridiculous to sit still in light of everything you feel you need to do. When you first start practicing, don't be surprised if boredom quickly sets in and your mind races or jumps from one thought to another in rapid-fire succession. You may only be able to stay still for a moment with each second seeming like an eternity, but that's O.K.

Keep practicing. Keep your mind quiet. Over time you may find that quieting the mind through the many acts of meditation, long walks, deep breathing or taking the time to get quiet in a hot bath becomes an essential and integral part of your life.

When my world was in total chaos, the advice to get quiet felt right. Now years later, I am constantly reminded that I can only experience the very nature of who I am when I am quiet and my mind is at rest. This occurs most readily in the early morning. It also sometimes occurs late at night after I have tired of the day's multitude of activities.

Quiet time allows the mind and heart to meet in the middle of thought with a tug of war. Which will win? The mind wishes to control while the heart seeks to expand. Once the intellect registers the struggle between these two feelings, the choice to quiet the mind is made, which allows the heart to wander through the halls of imagination. The key to unleashing the imagination is a matter of making the choice between the mind and heart. This is not willed but rather allowed. I have come to recognize that the feeling of my mind's neutrality allows my heart to expand with a sense of freedom, excitement and adventure.

Discerning enough to put the mind to rest is the key to

realizing your freedom from fear. When you consciously choose to allow your heart to take the reins, it may feel as if you are physically stepping through a doorway into another world.

When my imagination enters into the recesses of the mind, my heart opens up. When this occurs, I am being shown what is possible if I allow myself to let go of my worldly fears, struggles and resistance to change. I have found that it takes much courage to follow my heart, but when I come back from that inner feeling of exhilaration, I know I have seen and felt the truth of who I am. After this period of quieting the mind, I can then begin or end my day with a renewed sense of optimism and fulfilled purpose.

You will experience what it is like to be in Source by how you feel. Once the inner noise has quieted and the thoughts of fear melt into the background, a welling of emotion may come over you as you feel an inner glow and a feeling of immeasurable joy and loving kindness that will touch your heart.

As you learn to witness your thoughts you can begin changing your perspective of your circumstances immediately by getting your mind to quiet. When you are in one of your most fearful states, just repeat to yourself that you are loved and fear cannot touch you. This is a simple process but takes much in the way of practice and patience. It is not a quick fix for your troubles today but is one that if incorporated into your daily routine will literally transform any disturbed state of mind into peace.

Another commonly used method of quieting the mind is deep breathing for energizing and relaxing the body. To begin, you may wish to first take a few slow breaths in rhythm with your normal breathing then work your way into a deeper pattern of inhale and exhale. As you do so, focus your awareness approximately six inches above the top of your head then bring your awareness down through the center of you and anchor your awareness within your heart as you continue to modulate your cadence of breathing. Throughout your meditation, continue breathing in this relaxed manner until you have completely surrendered to a deep sense of inner peace.

There are many techniques for bringing your awareness to a state of neutrality as you move energy through your physical vessel. There are pathways through your system that correspond to different parts of the body. Deep breathing can accelerate the rate of return and open energy centers that lie dormant while in other states of consciousness. The most established forms of breathing can be found in the Vedic traditions of Yoga and Eastern spiritual practices.

Quieting the mind over the roar of life is a challenge but well worth the effort, and training the mind to open your heart is the key.

3. Listen to your heart

Our higher self knows what is best and right and the way to tune into the soul is by learning to listen to your heart. It is a soft spoken, gentle kind of voice that always prompts you to do what is in your best interest. The mind is constantly focused on what societal expectations are or what old unresolved programming dictates. It is also enmeshed in past misgivings. Intuition is directly connected to your heart center and in tune with the vibration of love, the kind of divine love that is directly in alignment with your soul's highest expression.

We actually have two hearts; one is physical and one energetic. One is the beating thriving muscle that pumps the blood through the vessels and keeps the body alive. It is the center of all earth bound activity but therein also lies the heart of hearts. This is the energetic center of your physical being that can be located on the quadrant meridian grid found within the human energy system. This is the area directly below your physical heart just under your breastbone. You can locate this energy center by inhaling very strenuously and feeling the hollow of your abdomen when you release the oxygen just inhaled. It is a soft spot just below the cartilage that protects the heart muscle that joins the ribcage.

The heart of hearts can be accessed by simply intending it to be so, but it takes practice to listen to its more subtle prompts. This is especially important to understand because as you intend, your body or energy system within the body will also begin to react and to free itself from the confinements of beliefs that no longer serve you. This will push you to reconfigure how you position yourself in the world by challenging you to release your old way of making decisions with your head and begin taking the more subtle prompts from your heart.

After you have set your intent, the mind will want to hold on and protect you from some unforeseen enemy but your heart will begin to open and relax. This tug between the mind and your heart will go on until you have learned to listen to your heart over the noise of the mind. These seemingly opposing forces can work in harmony, and it is just a matter of assuring the higher mind, the protective part of the self, that you have nothing to fear.

This, of course, takes time if you are to go the long road to change. However, this is not necessary if you can suspend your belief in the time continuum. This is where an act of faith is required if you are to allow the sanctum of your heart access to the mind.

Life is about learning to love with an open heart, and your soul is tuned to this high vibration of joy. By listening and following the prompting of the heart, you are accessing the very source of your creation.

As you learn to quiet the mind, you can become more aware of the fear that is ruling your life and getting in the way of your ability to listen to your heart. When you are clear of inner noise, turmoil and the constant chatter of the mind, you are at the center of your creation.

You know you are listening to your heart when the mind comes to a place of rest. Your heart then opens to reveal a deep sense of peace. We each have experienced this kind of soul talk at one time in our lives or another. You may have to reach pretty far back to recapture this feeling, but it is there. It is the stuff of recognition that comes over you when you are not thinking about anything in particular or maybe sense a spontaneous feeling of happiness or an urge to do something that brings you joy.

Maybe you have been working on a problem you have been trying to solve or a situation that is giving you pain and anguish. Maybe it is the feeling that comes to you in the early morning hours when you are sitting quietly. If you allow your mind to fall away for just a moment, you will find it there, patiently waiting for you.

There are times when you just realize something for no apparent reason. This is the soul talking through the feelings of your heart. I have come to know this as my intuition or being in communion with my higher self. The tricky part though comes when you are using your mind to move through the world and not checking in with your heart.

The mind is meant for fervency, not for masterminding your life. The mind can never know all the inroads to expansive living because it is full of beliefs that serve as filters to your thoughts. Your heart may speak clearly to you but if you allow the mind to over ride your intuition, your sensitivity will dull. When this occurs you will eventually find yourself in a situation or circumstance that is less than optimal or headed in the wrong direction altogether.

I have been battling an overactive, doubting mind my whole life. My heart speaks clearly yet my mind is constantly stepping in to run with an idea while forgetting to check in and pay attention to my intuition. Before I know it, I am off on a tangent and in trouble again.

The mind doesn't like changing courses. It is focused on the goal of finishing the task. The heart moves and changes with any given situation. It is attuned to maneuvering the minefields of life in such a way as to outrun, outsmart even the most crafty of circumstances. The drawback to relying strictly on the mind is that it only sees, hears and is aware of a very limited part of the picture. The difference between the two is like running an obstacle course in the dark wearing sunglasses instead of night-vision goggles.

When this happens, just remember that life is about learning, learning to love more deeply, freely and unconditionally. This whole process is one that tears at the emotions each day with every unfolding. Each time you trip yourself up and get off course, pick yourself up, tune back into your heart and redirect your course of action accordingly.

Just remember that to reveal your true nature, the heart must be open. You always have access to Source but may decide to unconsciously give your power away to others by ignoring your ability to tap into your higher power. If you find yourself doing this, it is because you are incessantly seeking affirmation from others rather than relying on what your heart has already prompted you to do. Such doubting weakens your inner voice of reason and puts the mind back in control. This type of outer questing is a distraction when the answer is right within your very grasp. As you learn to trust your intuition instead of the seemingly outer wisdom of outside circumstances or others, your inner voice will only grow stronger.

Often times the course of action the mind wants to take is not at all what your heart has already decided. It is only after you surrender your heart to God that your world will begin to change.

4. Trust your inner knowing

The process of asking and listening to your heart will build up a sense of expectation within you. Over time and practice, you will gain confidence in your ability to discern your inner direction by listening more fully and completely. The heart and mind are designed to work in harmony—the heart is to lead the way as the mind discerns the path.

How do you know if what you are sensing is for your best and highest good? Learning to trust this inner prompting is especially difficult if you are one who absolutely needs proof for everything in life. Even with such clear inner guidance, you may still feel doubtful when something just sounds too good to be true. That is doubt creeping into your inner world and wreaking havoc with your heart. It's pretty clear when the mind is pulling and tugging at you because you become focused on what you *should* do. This is a direct tip-off that the mind or ego has kicked into gear and is interfering with your heart.

You can learn to trust your intuition by establishing a benchmark for how you feel when you are in *heart*. You will recognize that all decisions of the heart are unfettered by the feelings of fear. Given our human nature, these lower vibrations have a way of creeping in to disturb your peace of mind but in the inner sanctum of heart-based decisions you can feel there is peace. You can tell if the mind is engaged in wishful thinking because you are thinking and rethinking positions and choices. Where there is doubt, the mind is pushing for certain outcomes rather than merely allowing the intuition to expand into your consciousness.

You may find that, at times, you will make a clear unequivocal decision while in the feeling of peace, then later doubt and fear will rear up and cause you to spiral down into the lower states of consciousness. When this occurs, just get in touch with that inner feeling again.

I have found that some of my greatest teachers in this regard are the individuals who heed those subtle prompts and move through life with ease and grace. When Spirit speaks, they listen and their lives are so incredibly rich because of it.

As you begin to honor your intuition and take action accordingly, your ability to trust will only grow stronger. This learning process is like anything else; it takes practice. By listening and learning to trust your inner voice and taking action on the prompting from your heart, you will begin to say goodbye to fear.

By tuning into your intuition, you will tap into a whole host of higher knowledge whenever you need it. That is why it is so important to begin understanding and looking out for the more subtle feelings of the lower emotions. They can cloud your inner voice, but by paying attention and releasing fear-based emotions, your inner voice will only grow stronger.

5. Surrender your fears to God

The many facets of spiritual awakening occur in the midst of crisis or tragedy. Many do not awaken to the fact that there is something beyond the physical senses until they have experienced the phenomenon called terror.

There are many who escape this feeling altogether and go straight to God but in doing so unknowingly give their power away to some unseen force. These are the times when we are putting all our faith in God but are not taking responsibility for the hell we have created.

When terror strikes, you may do one of the following: fight, take flight, freeze or surrender. Fighting takes the form of beating whatever physical obstacles you are confronted with and many go this route, time and time again. If you go the route of bullying your way through life, it will work for many situations but it is like binding hand and foot while trying to walk a tight rope. In short, you can do it but it's a very limiting way to go.

You may think that taking flight by routing a path of escape is also an option to transcending fear, but it is not. It is a choice that buys time but does not break through the barrier wall that you will find yourself in when your world has turned to chaos. You may initially choose this way of denying the very existence of what is ailing you, but eventually you will recreate the same dynamic that *forced you* to make the decision to run in the first place. Life is like that; always recreating what is within you.

You will run, fight or deny your way through life until one day, you will have become so overwhelmed by fear that you have created a situation or an event that is bigger than you are. This forces you to get real and to admit that you are no match for the terror that strikes your heart and overwhelms the mind. When this occurs, you have finally led yourself to the fourth and final choice of surrender.

Even as you get quiet and come to grips with taking that big leap of faith, terror may strike your heart just thinking about the need to place your trust in something greater than yourself.

You try to make the best choices for yourself but when fear is in control you may not feel safe. You also may not wake up until something traumatic happens that forces you to begin acting on faith. The changes leading up to this time are *always* set into motion long *before* your life comes crashing down around you.

As you surrender, you might say a prayer that sounds more like a bargaining table tactic but that's O.K. It may go something like this; "If someone or something will come and save, rescue or deliver me from hardship or tragedy then I will do, be or get something in return."

When I reached this stage of no return in my life, I was so accustomed to relying on my own wits that I was not even sure I could trust anyone including myself. As I have explained earlier, even this trust was built on a rocky foundation.

When it became obvious that I had exhausted my effort to outrun my circumstances and when losing everything I held dear seemed eminent, I felt I had nowhere else to turn. I was so distraught that I called a dear friend and asked that he come and sit with me because I didn't even trust what I would do in the blackness of what I was feeling. In the middle of the night, with tears streaming down my face, he told me that I was the most arrogant, stubborn person he had ever met because he could see that I had not once thought about turning to God. His statement incited anger within me but made me stop and consider his words.

I finally acquiesced to his suggestion that I pray. When I begrudgingly spoke my prayer of surrender, it was full of doubt and defiance. I prayed to a God that I no longer knew, but I asked to be delivered from the state of confusion and trauma that was playing out in my life. By doing so, I promised to follow my direction from that day forward, on only one condition: I needed God to deliver the guidance to me in clear, concise and specific terms. I wanted no further confusion. If God would grant me this one qualifier, I bargained, then I promised to follow my direction to the letter. The next day I slept and woke up feeling more peaceful than I had in months.

Of course, just like any other deal there are two sides to everything. Each person's act of surrender is deeply personal and may come willingly, or not. Either way, we must weigh and measure the choice of living life in the *hell fires* of fear or to surrender to something greater than ourselves. I have found that the choice to surrender is the only path that leads to freedom.

What you are doing when you surrender is opening yourself up to receive love and guidance from your higher power. Surrender is an action-oriented choice, because you are not foregoing your resolve to face your fear but *are* asking for help.

Once you decide to surrender, you have acknowledged that the Divine knows more than you do about your situation. And what is God? The answer to this question is different for each and every one of us, but it is the act of surrender that sets this quest into forward motion.

As you say your own individualized prayer to this unforeseen, invisible force, you may feel yourself give in to the fear that has held you captive. Don't be fooled by this experience. You are not moving back into the chaos but are now beginning to release your fears and move out of this lower vibration. Before you do though, you are calling everything up for release so that love has a place to fill the void of your own understanding.

Without surrendering our fears to our greater self, we will continue to be steeped in "poor me" thinking.

6. Forgive and keep forgiving

The act of surrender is not fully complete until you are called to forgive. You may fear that when you finally acquiesce to forgiving yourself or another, you will shut down all your senses, passion and feeling for life, or will direct your rage and anger at yourself for being right back in the same spot you started. Or, you just may fear that life was all just an illusion and nothing had really changed about your situation. The shock of it may be more than you can bear.

If you are at this point in your thinking, you are not seeing clearly now and know in your heart of hearts *much* has changed. You are not the same person now you that you were before. However, you still have the same emotional elements at work and have therefore recreated a dynamic that is calling you to release the lower vibrations causing you to feel this way.

When this occurs, ask God to take care of your every need, then affirm to the Divine what you will give back in return for this nurturing. You have bought into the feeling that you are in a circle and you are not. You are revisiting these same dynamics *not* to hold onto them but to release them from your energy fields. Your soul is *not* calling you to turn away and cut off from your emotions but to *embrace* how you are feeling and make decisions accordingly. Your soul asks for release of the lower emotional states of emoting and is asking you to trust in the bigger picture.

If you choose to shut down now, you will only be repeating the same lesson but to a harsher degree. Ask your guides that they take charge of the situation as you move to release the feelings of anger and move to forgive. First, forgive others then work your way to see how you have created your outer reality. You will then be shown *why* you have created these feelings and situations within you and in your world. Only then will you be called to forgive yourself.

After recognizing the self-destructive patterns in your life, change will happen dramatically because you will no longer resonate with a state of confusion. Each time you feel fear, inwardly affirm your desire for help then surrender to whatever comes before you.

Just remember, you are not in a circle of learning, but a spiral and are being called to *release* the vibration that has brought you back to this state of emoting. That's it.

When fear returns in full force and you feel confused, hear your voice of reason and stop feeling that you are not getting what your heart desires.

A simple prayer may be this: "God, give me clear, unequivocal direction as you show me the way out of this difficult situation and reveal to me the way to my heart's desire. In return, I promise to stop the self-doubting and unforgiveness of self and others." Then go about your day.

I highly suggest you take all energetic blocks away from your heart and this includes how you feel that you have been hurt.

LET IT GO. LET GO OF ALL HURT, ALL SLIGHTS, ALL FEELINGS OF FEAR OF NOT GETTING WHAT YOU DESIRE. LET IT GO. KEEP WORKING ON IT UNTIL YOU DO.

We all make mistakes. Know that your reaction to the situation or circumstance is about *you* not about anyone else. Let others worry about their own stuff. Focus on yourself by dropping the hurt.

The more you block another from your life, the more walls you will place around your energy fields.

The wall of hurt comes down when you forgive.

Forgiving is the release mechanism of lower vibration. Ask yourself the question, what am I being called to forgive? Then put the question out of your mind and wait for the answer.

Whatever it is will come up in a swell of emotion or a revelation of what your learning is about. You may start with what others have done to you. When you get to a place of understanding of how you have created your own hurt and pain, and have also been part of the play that hurt others, then you know you have reached the core of what you are being called to forgive.

How do you actively forgive? Feel your way into what comes and let it go, forgive yourself then affirm the freedom you desire. Claim it by verbalizing something like this, but in your own words: "I celebrate my highest expression and release all aspects that no longer serve me."

Affirm your new vibration and move forward in this Light, and know it is complete. By affirming this truth, you are choosing to release the whole paradigm of fear.

The next time you enter into the same dynamic that brought you to this state of being, feel compassion for the other's humanness as you are forgiving your own blindness. You are resonating at the same vibration that brought this situation to you. God has brought it to you for healing. How can you heal old wounds if you shun and condemn? If you condemn another you are condemning yourself.

Just remember the reflection and feeling of what you see in another is what you do not yet acknowledge is inside yourself. That is why it feels like an assault, because someone or a difficult situation is showing you a part of yourself you are denying.

Compassion. Give it to the other and you will receive the same. As you forgive yourself in creating the pain and hurt in your life, you can see your own undoing and gain compassion for others. As you open your heart to both in the same vibration, it will provide space for others to also open.

Spirit brings us big clues to let us know when we are entering into a learning curve. For instance, if you are resonating at an abuse or victimhood frequency, your energy fields will be activated around another who also has this vibration in their fields. Spirit will give you the prompting for learning by communicating through feelings. If you are drawn to someone, but they make you feel less than joyous, God is giving you a big clue that something is amiss within you. Now you can take action by clearing your feelings about the person or situation. By doing so, you are also triggering the healing in the other. You do this by changing your base resonance by releasing the lower vibration from your energy field.

For me, this type of release is felt at first as a deep sadness accompanied by the revelation of how I have created such personal hardship. As I let myself go from the bondage that I have been holding others in, through an allowance of a deep sadness to wash over me, I release and let go.

Our lack of understanding is *always* the source of our own hurt. You know you have found the answer when you no longer find that you are angry at anyone or any circumstance. This knowing occurs because you realize the learning in what you have created.

If you feel your fear-based actions damaged a relationship or hurt someone, perhaps a note or call is in order once you understand the dynamics of your behavior, when you are ready. A heartfelt apology for the part you played is always helpful to the process of healing. Also, by sharing your revelations, it may stir learning in the other for bringing a mutual lesson to close.

As you practice this active form of forgiveness, it is also wise to affirm the desire you hold for yourself. These are the affirmations of what you are and the intentions you hold in your heart for the purpose of realizing your heart's desire. Affirmations and intentions, especially when you find yourself overcome by the circumstances and events in your life, serve as a tool for resetting the mind to work more in harmony with your heart. In Eastern cultures, affirmations are called mantras and are used as a way to focus on the heart for more fully opening to God. In Christian practices, the beautiful prayers, creeds and rosaries serve this very same purpose. The most important part of an affirmation is the words, *I AM*. Anything else that affirms your highest purpose is great!

Here are a few examples, but I encourage you to create your own:

"I am a child of God. I know fully and completely that my safety and well being is with God. I reside in the heart of God."

"I am at peace."

"I am loved beyond all human comprehension."

"I am an open channel for the free flow of God's love and blessings."

As you keep your focus on your highest resonance, you will naturally begin to open to new possibilities. As fear and anxiety resurface, surrender and forgive. When you do so, you are effectively saying to your soul, "I am ready to listen. I am ready to say goodbye to pain and suffering, to separation and denial. I choose to identify with the God essence that I am, which is love united with Spirit."

On the surface, it may appear that the two ways of learning are the same because the action is the same, but meet a person who is motivated to take action out of joy and you know you have met a very special person. Their inner glow is unmistakable. Their words and body language reflect the inner peace just as surely as if they were basking in the sun after a cloudy day. The difference is that their heart is open and they are listening to their inner voice. As they interact with the world, they are effortless in the way they move because they are so attuned to being guided.

How foreign this way of living must seem to those of us who struggle, calculate, plan, strategize and doubt ourselves at every turn. When living in tune with your heart, you are in harmony with who you are and you have nothing to prove.

As you work through the muck and mire of heavy emotions that are holding you in bondage, it is important to actively be on the look out and release any old patterns that make you feel heavy or hold you back. As you move through the process of releasing, forgiving and affirming your new vibration, you will shift from a feeling of heaviness to light-heartedness.

7. Make prayer an integral part of your day.

The latest findings in the field of quantum theory and recent translations of the ancient Dead Sea Scrolls challenge us to totally revise our notions about how prayer works. Prayer is not an act of asking, but one of invocation with a grateful heart.

With your intention, set your will to fully align with the greater will of the Divine. In doing so, you may wish to speak the words, "I align myself only with my highest good and the good of all in this matter;" then feel your heart's desire in the situation or circumstance. As you do so, visualize everything about what you see as you feel your way into the prayer. The point is to bring your total focus and awareness into the feeling that is invoked when you are experiencing it in your imagination.

As you do so, consciously set your intent into motion by seeing, hearing and feeling that you are there and now in the moment of your creation. Bless this feeling and give it over to God. Do not go back into the situation with your mind and project worry and doubt into it. Let it be. You will know that you have your answer when you experience the feeling you invoked during the prayer. It may take you much effort to relinquish your fear of failure, but you must release these feelings from your mind as they come up.

The act of prayer is a single act in a day-long string of activities. If prayer is to be put into motion, then it is your thoughts, words and deeds that are to be brought into harmony. When you begin aligning with your highest expression, it will become obvious when you are *not* in alignment because you will feel the difference. You will catch yourself thinking less than affirmative thoughts and you will find yourself engaged in wrongful behavior.

During my early awakening period when I was at the height of major anxiety, my minister suggested I put a rubber band around my wrist to remind myself to curb my doubting thoughts. Every time my mind wandered to my troubles, which were about a million thoughts per minute, I lightly snapped the band against my wrist. Even after this tool served its purpose, I wore it for over a year as a continual reminder for me to keep my mind focused on what I desired rather than what I feared.

You may seek solace in prayer, but the mind is to follow the command of your heart. Use the act of prayer to put your fears to rest by seeing, feeling and intending your heart's desire to be so. If you are to transcend your fears, you must do it yourself; no one else can do this for you. It is hard work, but the reward is living a life that is graced by joyful learning.

EXPERIENCING PRESSURE TO REALIGN WITH SOURCE

What is it here to teach?
What is it that I need to learn?

Guides: Emotional stress is a physical condition.
It has nothing to do with your divine nature.
You have identified with the physical and must release
this silly notion, that your source comes from the
physical. It does not.

Until you have firmly planted your mind and heart in the
Divine, your strife will continue.

It is necessary to correctly align your Self with your
intuition.

Listen to it carefully.
We will never steer you wrong.
We do not want you to suffer.
You are doing this to yourself.

Your life does not have to be full of strife.

We do not want you to suffer to the extent that you
cannot do your work.

What is my work?

Guides: Your work is to love humanity.
You must communicate to the masses that the love of
humanity is acceptance that they are of one mind.
This is a universal concept that is to be communicated.
Only when this is united with the masses, will our work
be complete. All hearts must be kindled and united with
the one divine Light.

It is time for humanity to recognize their Father, their
Mother, their divine source, which is unconditional Love.

—August 27, 1991

THE WILL OF GOD

The will of God is to love your fellow man as you love your God.

Life is to be lived to the fullest of grand possibilities.
You are not here for the sake of strife.
All beings are to live their life based upon the unspoken truth that life is to be lived to the fullest.

You are to go in peace my child. You are not to involve yourself in the ways of the world.

If the ways of the world conflict with your God-given direction, you are to follow God's laws, not the laws of man.

Do not be fooled into accepting the status quo.

You are not to involve yourself.

Be in the world but not of it.

Your desires must be curbed.

—Nov. 23, 1992
Sri Sathya Sai Baba

Where there is love there is life.

—Mahatma Gandhi

CHAPTER FOUR

EMBRACING THE CHANGE YOU DESIRE

*Manifesting our heart's desire depends
on the choice we make—
to remain in fear or to trust God.*

Strategies for Transforming Your Life

Incorporating the tools for overcoming fear into your daily life takes practice with an unshakable resolve to change, but you may also wish also to consider adopting a plan for transforming any fear, no matter how disturbing or intimidating, into an inner calm and peace of mind.

Transformation or positive change within the vast universe of consciousness occurs within the *still point* of the mind and heart. *Still point* is that state of being achieved only when all thought is void and all resonance is in heart. This more expansive way of living begins to occur when your heart opens wide to Source; God pours forth grace and infuses us with millions of tiny high vibrational patterns of light-wave frequencies. These high frequencies serve to clear the physical, mental and emotional blockages from our energy bodies. However this act of clearing occurs in union with Spirit, and only if we are in an open state of acceptance. God may grant us many gifts born

103

from Spirit, but if we do not accept them with an open heart, it is the same as not receiving them at all.

It is not enough to think, feel and push with the mind. The pureness of our heartfelt intent to surrender to something greater is what opens our hearts to experience the fullness of life. By doing so, we are giving our Guides the signal to push. It is as if, on cue, the angels push higher frequencies of Light into our human energy system to clear out what is no longer serving us. This is a very fluid process. The entire spectrum of light-wave frequency is fluid, but because many of us have become so accustomed to living in the vibration of fear, our minds have crystallized our belief in a physical reality that is limited only to what we can see, hear, smell, feel and taste. But there is more to our physical reality than these five ways of perceiving. In each case, the senses represent a finite spectrum of the senses.

The more you can relate to a new paradigm, that the universe is comprised of more than what you know, your imagination will open up to exploring and accepting a whole range of new possibilities. This more expansive way of perceiving is not based on calculating and memorizing facts, but on a state of mind and readiness to learn.

Each person will eventually come to his or her own conclusion about this fact. Reality, some will say, is what you make it. In part this is true. Our perception is not always the truth, and truth does not change—only our understanding of it.

The choice for change begins with an open willingness to accept that reality is more than the physical senses. Sit with this concept of *still point* that I have just described at the opening of this chapter. Work with it a bit and see what comes to you. You may also wish to ask your angels and Guides for a brief demonstration of lifting the veil for gaining a better understanding. They are much closer to the earth plane of reality and are prepared, in fact, delighted to assist you.

Every time you call upon Spirit for help and guidance, the love that pours forth usually comes forward in a way that is most joyous and playful. I have found that the angelic beings will often use humor as a way to teach. They like to poke fun at our human foibles, but all for the sake of learning.

In early 2000, an example of this occurred in my home during a silent meditation. At the start of the evening, each participant stated his or her intent for learning. A participant asked that her life be cleared of clutter. During the hour of silence she could not get settled and squirmed the entire time. Afterwards she described a feeling of itching all over to the point of extreme discomfort. As she spoke, I tuned into what was happening. I saw dozens of little elf-like creatures buzzing all around her clearing her energy fields. They jokingly called themselves the *dust busters*. When I described what I saw, she had to laugh at the absurdity of how Spirit delivered on her intention to clear the clutter from her life starting with her energy fields.

On another occasion, she mentioned that she could not see or feel anything of Spirit. Just then she sensed a shiver go through her body that felt like a breeze, but nothing about our environment had changed. I watched as Archangel Michael, standing close to 20 feet tall, brushed his beautifully energetic wing over her face as he sashayed by her, then stood behind her as we continued to visit. Her statement was dwarfed by the joy she felt in that moment.

After you have become practiced at quieting your mind and maintaining an open state of readiness, you may wish to

age in Spirit. For this purpose, you may inquire
Light being of the Angelic order to assist you.
nere is a brief guide:

1. Sit quietly in a comfortable chair or on the floor with your favorite pillow. Arms are to be relaxed at your side or on your lap. Palms facing in an upward open position but completely relaxed.

2. Back is to be straight. Sit up straight, erect but not tense.

3. Focus your attention within your heart of hearts. This is not a pushing, focused kind of feeling, but intended for *listening*.

4. Connect your heart while focusing on your third eye (the middle of your forehead, just above your brow). This feels like you are going to sleep. Before you give up the struggle to stay awake, relinquishing your body to sleep, there is a point when you release the body to Spirit. This is the feeling you are to connect with and to invoke. If you need a demonstration, merely watch your mind as you fall asleep tonight. You will get it very quickly because you do it all the time as a part of your sleep cycle.

5. Remain in this watchful, relaxed restful state and surrender to it fully and completely. By doing so, you are expanding your energy bodies out just as when you are sleeping, but now you are consciously awake.

6. While in this state, simply hold your question in thought and wait.

7. Within this *still point* of watchful repose, your angels and Guides can communicate with you. They will envelop you with their energy fields and transmit light wave frequencies that will send you into a state of bliss. They will share insights by speaking to you by way of intuitive receivership which is experienced through feeling, imagery and smell.

8. As you practice this state and remain open, you will begin to ask for and receive assistance as a part of your daily life.

There is a wondrous feeling of love and kinship waiting to be expressed through the heart of God. I liken it to a team of astronauts embarking on a mission. We are the astronauts up in space, but we have forgotten that our ground crew, our angels and guides are here to help us. They are here with us at all times, but when we are engulfed in fear, we feel we are all alone and sometimes only tethered to Source by some distant remembrance, feeling or impression. Our angelic helpers and teachers know everything about us and are here to guide us. We simply need to ask them for help.

The Strategies

I don't know about you, but when I am lost and feeling out of sorts, I pick up a book or call a friend to find a way to remedy my feeling of confusion or work through a difficult challenge. Life is meant to be shared as we work through our learning, but sometimes we just need a push to get us started in the right direction.

The strategies that follow are that kind of push—just a nudge here and there to ask that you consider seeing your life and your challenges in a different light. I am discovering that the bulk of my roadblocks come from my mind. As I believe, I create. As I feel, I see life in terms of those feelings.

Consider employing these techniques when life gets rough, or consider them when you are feeling unenthusiastic. Take what you like and leave the rest, or adapt your own version of this same philosophy and apply the parts that make the most sense.

1. Live life in the moment

Living life in the moment is the only thing you will find that brings the greatest degree of satisfaction. If you keep your mind mulling over past misgivings or regrets, you are holding onto old energy of conflict and pain. Likewise, when you are so focused on your future, you are not allowing the space for enjoying the learning of the day. By missing the moment, you relive your past and may even thwart your future. The inner prompting from the heart of God speaks to you when you are experiencing life in the immediate present.

Each moment of stillness provides your heart with a way to connect with the Source of your creation. In many ways, you do this all the time. The difference is that when you listen to the inner prompting and take action, you begin to jump from the treacherous flow of fear into the direct current of Love. Love unites the heart and mind into one body of synchronistic wave pattern and expands your auric field outwardly.

2. Set your intention to realize your heart's desire

Your life is a product of your creation and you have created everything out of the beliefs that you hold. This creates a field of energy as you influence interactions and events in your life. If you are holding onto hurt and pain, or denial of self-love, then you are acting like a giant magnet for attracting similar experiences to you. These lower vibrational frequencies create a field of influence that resonate with others who are feeling the same.

Your process of self-discovery can be accelerated as you more fully connect with God. You do this by listening to your heart as you continue to clear old beliefs. The feeling of being in

Source or remaining rooted solely in the physical can be likened to listening to the music of Mozart versus heavy metal. One is melodic and the other jarring. When there are energy blocks in your fields of influence, your intent bounces from block to block and either does not reach its destination or succumbs to a belief. Just realize that behind or around that belief is a grid system that will deliver the most delicate melodies of the heart to its intended destination.

Manifestation comes when the heart is fully open and in alignment with Source. As a result of maintaining an openness to Source, you are freer to clear the filters caused by beliefs as you follow the direction set by your soul.

The human energy system is part of a vast grid system that is a different kind of communication road map. It is comprised of electro-magnetic fields that connect you to everything everywhere simultaneously. The grid system traverses the universal life force fields of thought and works through intent. When your energy bodies ignite into a quickened expansion, you are literally tapping into and becoming fully enmeshed in the grid. As you do so, you will gain access to a vast array of knowledge as you transform your physical form into the higher patterns of Light.

What makes this happen? It happens when your heart is open and your intent is pure. When both are in place, your energy bodies are aligned with God's will rather than getting mired in confusion and indecisiveness brought on by fear. With this connection, your intent moves through the grid system at lightening speed with pinpoint accuracy. There are no guitar riffs in the elaborate music of your soul's highest expression.

Your alignment with God is what sets manifestation into motion and fully engages you with the grid system. Then, by taking actual steps, you are providing the locomotion for realizing your heart's desire in worldly terms. This is when the connection with Spirit comes in. Your angels and Guides provide the navigational direction for operating in the world.

You may not be able to see what is in front of you at this point, but you can feel what your heart is discerning. These impressions, hunches and promptings from Spirit provide the tools for transforming your life into dreams that become a reality. When you realize your heart's desire, you recognize you have held these impressions as heartfelt remembrances your whole life.

Become more comfortable with setting your intentions and aligning with Source to access the grid system. As you practice integrating this into your life, you will come to a place of thoughtful contemplation and begin opening your heart more fully to God.

3. Change what you create by choosing differently

When you have created a situation or circumstance that is less than desirable, has backfired altogether, or is eerily like something that has occurred before, you are once again faced with your worst fears. Recognize that you are still steeped in the learning and choose to react to your circumstances differently. Your fears will trigger you to reconsider the visceral feelings you are experiencing from this sense of deja vu, but step back from the emotions for a moment and ask why.

The very nature of life dictates that you make a choice to remain in this state of being or change the way you react to outside stimulus. In fact, the emotion of fear is for the express purpose of pushing in on your auric field. This field comprises layers of energy bodies that can be described as balloons filled with helium. They are light and full of buoyancy; however, the physical world is a mix of lower vibration like dense cold air, acting as blinders. I say lower because the very physical dense matter that we see as a chair or table is the same dense matter that pushes into our auric balloon. The trick is to rise above and avoid deflation.

We cannot see who we are until we understand who we are not. We are not fear and we are not victims of our circumstances.

I do not use the word "control" lightly. We are in part controlled by our physical circumstances. These circumstances take form as our living conditions, geographical location, the work we desire, our loved ones and the greater cosmos. However, we can change our environment by focusing our intent on what we desire by feeling and being it in the moment. An example of how to do this is being researched by the work of Dr. Emoto.

Dr. Emoto, a scientist in Japan, is conducting research to prove that our thoughts and feelings can command the very nature of our physical reality. He has coined the term *hado* to describe an intrinsic vibrational pattern at the atomic level in all matter, the smallest unit of energy. Its basis is the energy of human consciousness. His theory postulates that, since all phenomena is at heart resonating energy, by changing the vibration we change the substance.

To explore his theory further, Dr. Emoto and his supporters successfully carried out a dramatic demonstration of *hado* in action on the shores of Lake Biwa, in the Kansai area in Western Japan. By holding the intent to purify water, about 300 people sent out thoughts imbued with a specific declaration. As the growing season approached, they observed that an aquatic plant, which was the source of a foul odor, never grew back again. The lake was transformed into a clean state. Dr. Emoto has gone on to photograph frozen water crystals. With the aid of a camera powered microscope, as people spoke different words into water molecules he froze them instantly. The photographs revealed that each word created a different crystal pattern in the water molecule. Love was the most beautiful and complex.

The Spiritual Guides tell me that each of us create our own reality, and our belief in a static physical world dictates that we are controlled by it. In the larger scheme of things, as a soul force, we group together with other souls prior to birthing into physicality, but before we do, we each decide how we wish to learn. This learning resonates at a particular vibratory pattern.

For example, a soul may wish to experience forgiveness more fully and will therefore select a soul group, during a particular incarnation, with a primary resonance of hate. During the individual's lifetime, the focal point of one's learning may be to more fully accept and express unconditional love.

Our souls set the lower personality self up to experience a variety of emoting states for the express purpose of releasing fear from our energy fields. This releasing process shifts our physical beings into higher frequencies of Light. In order to do so, we create life circumstances that enhance the higher vibrations of love or force us into the lower states of emotional turmoil. In a way, it's all a cosmic game of choice.

The emotional states of fear trigger the emotions to manifest chaos for this sole purpose; to get us to make a choice between spiraling down into the lower states of fear or transcending this chaotic feeling and transmuting the emotion to a higher vibrational frequency or wave pattern of Light.

You can visualize this process as an ocean wave of your thoughts and feelings crashing upon the beach of your outer world while the dominant ocean tide of Spirit pulls and pushes the larger bodies of water. The ocean depths are the vastness of your soul. Every person represents a micro version of the entire system of ebb and flow pushing from Spirit. Why? To learn how to love more deeply, fully, compassionately and openly.

As you become more akin to this tide changing your life, you will recognize the source of your creation as you make "best" and "right" choices. While in the vibration of fear, you are pushing against the tidal current, so to speak. The ocean of humanity is *love*, not fear. Therefore, by learning to resonate more fully with love, the issues of fear that cause you so much difficulty will quickly dissipate and melt into the ocean of the Divine.

Another step in this unfolding process is making the choice to let go of your identification with pain and suffering. Once you have recognized the need to do so, and have surrendered your fears to God, you have taken another positive step toward realizing your freedom.

4. Maintain a state of open watchfulness

When confronted with emotional stress, our human nature is too quick to spiral downward into a state of fear. You can learn to maintain an open state of watchfulness by calling on and tapping into Spirit to guide you. By doing so you will forever change your concept of openness. This state of being feels like a cavernous feeling of joy, and is realized as you open your heart fully to Source. It occurs when you are in touch with your heart's desire. This is the kind of desire that can only be felt and is deeply personal.

When immersed in this feeling, you will discover your divine nature. The very essence of your divinity cannot be compared to worldly feelings, but when accessed through the recesses of your heart, the mind-body connection will dissipate. The many nuances of joy are felt while in a state of ecstasy.

Ecstasy is the closest resemblance to the feeling of Spirit. However, the subtleties and over-riding quality of this emotion is not like the physical fibrillation of sexual energies, but is experienced as heightened states of awareness. This awareness is not one in which the mind is at the forefront of your consciousness, but where it relaxes into the recesses of the heart.

When you are consciously in Source, your heart opens and reveals much in the way of awareness that is likened to abandoned joy. This is purely an expression without words. In fact, words are chunks of gargled intonations that are no match for the infusion of audio, visual and clairvoyant perceptions of God when you are at the very center of your creation. Each energy wave contains more information than today's high-speed computer chips and more richness than all the tones in a symphony. Connecting to Source through your heart allows you to experience God as a state of being.

The key to maintaining this state is your acceptance of Spirit into your inner sanctum of thought and feeling. You can allow this by intending it to be so. This is not to say that you do not allow your mind to function in your day-to-day awareness of life awakenings. You most certainly do. In this *heart* state of being, you are commanding your way into a higher vibratory pattern of living as you act on the prompting of your heart. I am using the word *living* as an extension of your *being*. As your actions begin to reflect more and more your state of being, you will begin to more fully integrate the higher vibrations that you are into your physical expression. Maintaining this kind of open mindset is what allows, by the grace of God, to fill the void of your understanding, which flows more Light into your physical body.

5. Release all beliefs that are rooted in fear

While in this state of open readiness, you can create the manifestations of your own desire. As you desire, you are also placing your full unadulterated trust in God. This trust is not one that gives your power away to someone or something outside yourself. It is important to correctly position your spiritual center in a state of open watchfulness by acknowledging that you are a creator capable of manifesting your heart's desire.

The spiritual law of oneness states that you are one with everyone and everything. You are also that which has been created for your learning. Therefore, as you command your divine nature into higher physical expressions of your own divinity, on the soul level, you are the one who is calling you to change.

When looking at this from a vertically aligned perspective, you will see this is true. Just as I used the astronaut-to-ground-crew explanation, this concept is a matter of feeling the vibration that you are. You are that which you have created. *You* are more than the personality and the physical body. You are more than the mind. While your intellect and your ability to reason is fully associated with the mechanics of the brain, it is also directly linked to Source.

As you call your higher self forward, vibrationally, you are actually working in a vertically aligned stream of consciousness. As I mentioned earlier, fear is a lower frequency of energy and is vibrating at a slower rate of speed. This also equates to the resonance of the physical body. If your energy bodies are heavy-laden with fear, you are vibrating at a lower resonance than the highest expression of your soul.

An example of this alignment can be likened to a diver feeling the weight of water. The diver feels that his body is heavy when he is just below the water's surface but lighter as he descends to the depths. It is the same body of water but the deeper he goes, the freer he feels. In a vertical alignment with Spirit, our lower self is full of heaviness yet our souls are made of the same God essence. As we release the heaviness of fear, our load of life becomes lighter.

When you set your intent to merge your lower self with the higher part of your soul, you will begin to shed the many skins of blocked energy to more fully merge with who you truly are. After you have cleared the debris that holds you down, your higher vibratory resonances will begin to merge more completely to create a continuous column of Light. You certainly have a choice in how you will experience this alignment process—by remaining in the physical while raising your vibration, or leaving the physical vessel altogether and returning the body to dust.

6. Choose to align with your soul's purpose while you are still using fear as a motivator

This way of feeling your way through your fear is for the express purpose of releasing the beliefs that create a feeling of heaviness, and to keep your mind forever focused on your limitations. If you are to fully understand your heart's desire in the still point of the moment, your intent is to be set for vertically aligning with your soul's highest expression.

Your soul's purpose can be defined as *highest*, or *best* because there simply is no other alternate feeling in which to describe something without limitation. Anything less than a label of *highest* or *greatest* in our English vocabulary is very limiting and confines the energy fields to a qualifier. If you allow your heart to open, you will experience your world as a playground of pure joy.

There is no qualifier on your soul's ability to evolve and to merge with the Divinity that you are. As you practice aligning your energy fields in a vertical formation, you are in actuality widening the channel of your heart of heart's to more fully open to Source. This allows a fluid interchange between you and your soul.

There are many who will remember the beginning of their earth bound quest during this time of choice-making. However, it is not necessary to remember former-life experiences in order to remain in an open state of awareness. If you are living moment to moment, in feeling, the very nature of past and present is something of a misnomer. Time is not the metered clock we have created it to be. In actuality it is as fluid and relational as the energy of creation. Humanity has merely created a perception of time that conforms to our belief in the physical laws of nature.

As you practice this state of being, you will notice your sense of time shift and change in ways that allow the mind to expand. You will also begin to create a sense of awareness that prepares you to adjoin with others who have garnered a mode of living that is not unusual for the times. These are the souls who, as they have surrendered to the will of God, have landed squarely at the foot of change. By embracing the challenges put before them, they have set standards of achievement. As you call your higher-self forward, change is now welcomed not feared. If you are willing to give up your belief in fear and embrace love as the creator of your world, then hang onto your hat and be prepared to enjoy the ride of a lifetime.

7. Practice Acceptance

Humankind has spent trillions of dollars exploring the outer reaches of the universe and has made great strides in discovering the world in which we live, but their is an entire galaxy of Light within us and beyond anything the most powerful telescope can find. We are, in fact, a small part of the vastness of life called God's kingdom. I use this term religiously in one sense and profoundly in another, for there is no ample description to encompass any one explanation about the world in which we live. While spiritual seekers sense the cosmos, scientists explore and measure the enormity and complexity of physical matter as we know it.

Even with discerning between two divergent perspectives, when it comes to reality, it is still like trying to describe the whole elephant when you can see only a limited view. It is all a matter of perspective. When you are at the elephant's tail and see only its hindquarter, your viewpoint is partial. Someone may ask about the trunk but you will then have to ask, "Trunk? What trunk?"

How does this analogy apply to life and learning? It is the same with accepting differing perspectives as a way of living. The human experience is a part of the vastness. We are surrounded with much mystery and exploration, yet we each choose to see life from a narrow slice of reality. There may be a whole world out there, but gaining those extra few minutes of sleep before catching a train or bus to start the day may be the only priority that holds any relevance at that given moment. This analogy parallels the act of accepting another's viewpoint. When our reality of a situation, opinion or way of living collides with others, life can get pretty sticky.

Looking at the issue of acceptance from the soul's perspective as pure learning, there is no right or wrong. We are engaged in experiential learning. If we consider this as a viewpoint, then everyone is right in the way they experience their world.

If you accept this basic theory as the soul's way of learning, then you may also consider acceptance of another's viewpoint as a way to operate within *our* world. This is where the benefit of working through the heart comes into play. Rather than getting caught up in how you are positioning yourself in the world, which is strictly a structure of the mind, you can feel your way into love and acceptance.

When you are operating in *your* world, you are right about everything in it. When we are operating in *our* world, then acceptance would seem the most logical approach. By accepting another's perspective, you are not saying that you agree or follow whatever path they have chosen, you are acknowledging that you accept *their* view of the world for *them*.

But what happens when two perspectives come colliding into *our* viewpoint? For instance, you feel that a friend has kept a secret from you and violated your trust. Yet your friend values confidentiality and does not freely share what others may want to know. Who is right?

This shared experience happens when two or more are gathered in God's name. What does this mean? It means that when we are gathered in the presence of one another, we are to realize that there is something greater at work here than individual viewpoints. We recognize that no one person or group has the whole picture. Using the analogy of trying to understand the trunk of the elephant when you can only see the hindquarter, you are acknowledging that you cannot see the *whole* elephant.

When acceptance is put into practice in daily life, the sacredness of God can be felt through relationships, a smile, a handshake, or a touch. Life becomes a bit gentler to the senses because we are knowing and appreciating other viewpoints. Acceptance is a rare commodity in today's world, but is an essential ingredient if you are to feel your way into higher vibratory patterns of being.

The greatest act of acceptance is acknowledging that we are a part of the very God to which we pray. In the *Life and Teaching of the Masters of the Far East*, by Baird T. Spalding, Jesus is quoted as saying, "Ye are Gods and sons of the most high." The Guides have also affirmed that "We are God incarnate in physicality." Over the years, I have been working to reconcile these teachings with my traditional Judeo-Christian upbringing and have come to recognize that as I believe, I create. The first law of creation is *God* and the first words are *I AM*. These are very powerful words that I have come to accept as key teachings for realizing my soul's highest vibration. Through the many energetically delivered lessons, I realize that we are *all* Divine beings who have forgotten the source of our very own creation. I have no logical proof for this statement, only a deep sense of knowing that this is truth.

As you begin to shed fear-laden beliefs, you will transcend self-imposed limitations and realize that acceptance of self, your

God self, is the greatest gift that you can give is to share with another. If you experience anything less than who you are, you have misidentified with the very source of your creation.

8. Seek out spiritual role models

It takes courage to make changes in our lives. To make the determination to change is one thing, but it takes guts and resolve to follow through as you take action. Peer group pressure is tough on teens. You may be able to relate to that. Adults suffer from the societal *get ahead blues*. It is a very intense cycle that escalates once you reach that magical state of adulthood when the job brings the money; the paycheck buys the car, a house and the family begins to grow.

It's unending and a heavy responsibility that is felt by all who tread the expected path of social and economic ascension. Many of us know how to move forward, to go up, but what about coming down? Our American work ethic and psyche doesn't allow for this. Relatively few who have dropped out of society come back to the inner circle of upward mobility to tell about it. They usually form their own brand of community and begin to build a counter culture of sorts. An example in recent American history was the cultural revolution that started in the early 1960s. Many individuals rather than follow the example of their elders, set out on alternate life paths.

That is the way it is with us humans, forever forming groups or tribes for the sake of gaining an illusionary feeling of safety and security. When we are faced with the challenge to change, we are called to transform. This kind of metamorphosis is a personal journey and no one can do it for you.

The one thing I have found with any kind of life transition, is that these times do not necessarily have to be painful, especially if the path has been paved by someone before you.

These individuals can be spotted because they appear out of nowhere to say a kind word, offer to help or just accept where you are when you feel like doing nothing but crying. They are also the ones who step in at a moment's notice when emergencies strike or who prompt you to rise to your soul's challenge.

During times of turmoil, you may get so immersed in the change process that often these individual acts of kindness are lost to the many swirling difficulties that arise. Yet in the quiet of your heart, you know that you are witnessing a role model in action. You can spot these spiritual warriors, individuals who open their hearts to others for the sake of serving the greater good, by the very feeling they invoke within you. This feeling warms your heart and creates an oasis of calm in the midst of stormy emotions.

As you learn to change with the tides that move and push you to look inward, their leadership can help you to overcome the emotion of chaos, stress and strain. As you come through the storm, you may even come to realize the many acts of kindness that have helped to push you to see who you really are. You may also come to cherish the many friendships you are bound to make, as you work to overcome some of your greatest life lessons.

9. Choose how you will learn

You can determine your path, your way of living, by the outer prompting that leads you to a higher purpose. You can also undergo surgery of sorts and experience the kind of trauma that molds and shapes your thoughts, feelings and perceptions of life, which will change your spiritual landscape. Both are valid choices. Either way, you are bound to encounter obstacles along the way.

How you live is a choice, but by listening to the inner prompting of life's direction, you are choosing to follow an easier route. By making joy your guide, your journey will become more synchronistic and orchestrated. The other way will get you to the same destination, but will be wrought with roadblocks.

After you set your intent, if you are not taking full responsibility for your actions, Spirit will put a person or situation in your path as a challenge. When this occurs, you can rise to the occasion or move into a downward spiral of learning. The way to reset your intent is to compare your feelings about what is happening, at this point in time, with the intention you first put into motion. By discerning the difference between the two feelings, you will realize that this challenge, which on the surface may seem harsh, actually gives you exactly what you intended. Just remember, your soul gives you this opportunity to embrace the path to higher learning.

Our culture is famous for being steeped in victim consciousness, which manifests as giving our power away. The dialog may sound like this, "I *always have to do it* but *they* never have to", or " I didn't have any other choice; *they made me do it*." There are many derivatives of these two statements, but the core belief is one of victimhood. You may be experiencing this vibration and not even realize it on the conscious level. However, the way to discern whether you have bought into this belief is to monitor your thought patterns and words, as needed. Believing that you are somehow a victim of your circumstances, or that life is unfair, holds you down and keeps you away from experiencing the very essence of joyful living.

10. Set goals by putting your faith in God

Goal setting is a fabulous tool and I use it all the time. However, I have learned that the traditional ways of planning set me up for living in a feeling of lack or never quite making it.

In our worldly way of living, there is always something left undone, something not quite right, a skill to perfect or someone to please. The trouble with this mode of planning our way through life is that no matter how lofty the goal, we are always striving to perfect something for the sake of making us feel whole. This is a fear-driven way of getting ahead when, in fact, we are expecting ourselves to either fail or to *never* get it right.

Perfection, where human nature is concerned, is an oxymoron. We are human and were never designed to be perfect in the way we have set ourselves up to be. It is like holding a carrot out in front of a horse's nose just enough out of reach so that he will follow it anywhere. Our total focus is on getting that juicy orange treat. No matter how pure our intentions or how fool proof our plan, we are destined to stumble and fall short of our lofty goals somewhere along the way. Then we kick ourselves for not quite measuring up, or allow others to reinforce how we did not quite deliver on our promise to ourselves to be perfect.

How often do you push yourself for the sake of obtaining some predetermined goal, only to find that you never really get to eat the carrot. You may have so focused your attention on the reward in front of you that you are oblivious to everything else around you.

The real tragedy in life is that when we awaken, we may realize that we have spent much time, money and emotional capital on a way of being that makes absolutely no sense with no lasting intrinsic value.

I'm not saying that goal setting should be tossed out the window, but as you jump from the turbulent waters of fear into the gentle flow of love, you may wish to consider changing your definition of a goal. In spiritual terms, goal setting is like a football. It has a specific shape and property to it, but once it is airborne, its forward thrust into the winds of change impact where you will land.

You can set a goal, put your best foot forward, then trust that the forces of nature have as much influence over your direction as you do. It's important to remember to relax and enjoy the process of learning that ensues once you throw your goal into the winds of change.

The fuel that ensures your goals will be met, beyond your expectation, is intent. Before you do anything, set your intent for your realizing your greatest and highest expression, then put your faith in God and follow your soul's intuitive prompt.

When in touch with your heart's desire, strife and worry over life is removed to reveal a most marvelously synchronistic adventure. When goal setting this way, your life will become full of lusciously, gracious, laughable, silliness, only God could conjure up, on a clear blue-sky kind of day.

11. Shed the beliefs that rule all closed learning behaviors

The Spiritual Guides say that once we are awakened to our highest expression, but then begin to backslide into fear by incessantly asking questions, or remember our past misgivings with such fervency, or loathing our future awakenings, we are essentially deadening our senses to the divine guidance given to us so freely.

If you find yourself back in a state of fear and self-doubt after you have recognized the signs, then you are not trusting that your soul is in charge of your awakening. There is a big distinction between asking your Guides for help to gain further understanding or to gain a different perspective, and asking them to live your life or take control and tell you what to do. Self-doubting is buying into the illusion of not being Divine.

If you have a pattern that makes you spiral into self-destructive thoughts that are not productive and find you are isolating yourself from joy, you are sitting in doubt and remorse, which gets you nowhere. This state of being kills the spirit of self love and closes the heart into itself. It is worse than sitting in unknowing because you are applying the backwards laws of nature. Nature dictates expansion and growth or death and recycling to create new life.

Any dark-night-of-the-soul should not turn into weeks, months or years. I am only now fully understanding that the many long periods of hovering on the edges of depression over past circumstances is what kept me in this state for so long.

Self-perpetuating any and all inner turmoil and self-doubt keeps us in the same energy as if we were still back in the original state of fear that pushed us into our awakening to Spirit. If the nuances of fear are not cleared from your energy fields, you will recreate the same dynamics of fear over and over again until you wake up and command your life to take a different direction.

How does one get unstuck or climb out the halls of guilt? It is not necessary to feel this way when you are trying to find your way through the maze of learning. Just look around you and you will find peace of mind. It is found by kindness not

126

harshness, love not hate, joy rather than tears of discontent. The choice is for life over death, the kind you can find only by awakening to the God being that you are.

As you keep your heart open to Spirit, there comes a time when you are prepared to fully face your fears. Just as there are troubled outer worlds, inner worlds can also be a very scary place. In the sanctum of thought, there is a part of the self that disengages in the reality we create because we are afraid of facing the terrors that frighten us so.

At some point in time, your inner being may say, "I am not afraid anymore." This is often a small voice that comes from deep within the recesses of your heart. The mind is still very busy covering what the heart already knows. The mind controls this part of your inner being and tries to keep the body-mind belief going for the purpose of self-protection. As long as the mind is fully focused on outside stimulus for discerning your life direction, the heart cannot be heard.

It takes an act of courageous recognition to throw off the illusions that the mind has created. It's a pretty scary, threatening, intimidating world as far as the mind is concerned. The heart most certainly knows better, but is no match for the mind when fear evokes us to take action. As we learn to change our patterns, we will attract different experiences to us.

This is exactly what happened in my life, just four years after I left the ruins of my former life, I realized I was manifesting the same feelings of fear but to a lesser degree. Even though I was moving forward, (I had a new job I loved, a safe environment for my children, a wonderful man in my life with a house in the Maryland suburbs), I was still sitting in the energy of self-judgment for the life-choices I had made. I was still living out my day-to-day existence in the energy of caution, protectionism and guilt, and was playing out my belief in duality in grand style. No matter what I said or did, this energy was still being reflected back to me in my personal and professional relationships.

The pivotal point my life's direction came suddenly one evening, when after attending a friend's funeral, all the emotional confusion I had been so embroiled in since making the move north on the promise to remarry, hit me full-force in the gut. In the stillness of my heart I fully recognized that I needed to, once again, take charge of my own happiness. With this knowing, I was faced with the challenge of honoring my inner most desire to live fully by honoring my faith. With the resolve to make a change for the better, my life's direction, once again, began to shift.

Several years later, with both my teens out of high school, I returned to Fredericksburg with a heartfelt desire of living my life centered in Spirit. I found myself deciding to purchase the very first house my son and I looked at, just north of the city of Fredericksburg. As I settled in, I began to see the results of God's love manifest in new friendships, a professional change of direction and spiritual awakenings that were nothing short of profound.

The story, above, is an illustration of setting an intent based upon an inner knowing, then matching that 'like'"vibration with another. It is called the law of attraction which is the law of your being. It is not good or evil, moral or immoral. It is simply a blind law that always cooperates in perfect accord with what you command. It is the one source of perfect justice, and by its action you reap what you have sown. The standard that you measure others by is measured back to you equally. There is no way to escape this law. You are using it consciously or unconsciously. It is the law of life and controls the universe with absolute undeviating precision and justice.

So how do you shed the beliefs that rule your behavior? You are God incarnate in physicality yet the very nature of stepping up to claim your birthright scares even the most courageous divine being.

It requires an act of self-acceptance, which is a simple process, and just like the forgiveness of others, there will come a time in your awakening that you will be called to forgive yourself for causing so much pain and hardship to yourself and others in your state of unknowing. For me, this was the hardest part of my journey, but one that was key to forgiving myself.

When you are ready to face this aspect of your learning, you will know it because you are diligently working through releasing past pains and patterns that no longer serve the intentions you have set. Just remember; it's O.K. to be scared. As you work to acknowledge your humanness, you are also to affirm that you are a powerful being of Light who is now in charge of your journey.

When I was steeped in fear, I was totally convinced that there was no other way out of the loop unless someone or something came to show me the way. The very act of God as an outside appeal rendered me completely powerless and helpless in every sense of the word. It took years of working through the many emotional traumas caused by my own denial of self until I woke up to the realization that I was the one who had to take charge of my happiness.

Strange as this may seem, I have met many, since the time of my own rude awakening, who honestly believe that their spouses, friends, siblings, employers, the government or some outside, unseen force is responsible for their happiness or the grief

129

they are experiencing. Until or unless you are willing to address and accept this part of your learning, you will continue to manifest a mixed pea-soup bag of situations and circumstances in your life.

Self-acceptance challenges you to assume full responsibility for your creation. This includes anything you have perceived up to this point in time—whatever you feel others have *done to you*. Just remember that you are the creator of everything in your life. There is no exception to this truth. You are most definitely the product and result of your own actions. To say anything less is believing that you are less than a powerful creator.

You may choose to reside in ignorance, but this does not mean that you are any less powerful when unconscious of your manifestations. You may be asking at this point in time, "If I am such a powerful creator then why would I choose to struggle or to be so unhappy?"

The answer is found in the process of learning. That is why we each decide our learning before we are born into the physical reality of worldly vibratory patterns. You decide in your microcosmic way which emotions of frenzy you will be contributing to the whole of humankind. On the soul level, in the instant of birth, you pull the veil of understanding down around your divine consciousness to effectively lay the groundwork for an enriched life of learning.

You can also choose the way you wish to learn. If you are reading this book, then you will to be asked as a seeker of higher truth, at some point in time, about your resolve to remain in a state of unknowing or to transcend the cyclical method of learning the hard way. You may wish to pause now and affirm your desire to awaken.

If you answered affirmatively (yes, I would like to transcend any and all states of my own unknowing), your decision to shift out of the state of veiled consciousness will put two things into motion:

1. Your energy fields will begin to transmute the vibrations of fear into the higher vibrations of love.

2. You will begin to experience physical, emotional and mental delusional realities for clearing the fields of distorted beliefs and unnecessary characteristics.

The delusional characteristics that you carry within your auric field may be weighed down with disturbing memories from the culminated experiences of learning. As you clear your energy bodies, the intensity of the release may call forth powerful imagery and emotions that may at times feel overwhelming and without a reference point. When this occurs, simply acknowledge and think or speak an affirmation acknowledging its release. An affirmation such as, "I release all lower vibrations and embrace all that I AM" works to reset the mind and transmutes the lower vibrations of thought wave patterns into higher vibrations of love.

While still in a state of unconscious thought, as your heart begins to open, affirm that you wish to release the physical confinements of your fears. As you do so, you are now earnestly attempting to transcend your own limitations. You may invoke your angels and Guides to help you begin to energetically *shift* that, at times, may test your very sanity.

As you begin to consciously release the illusions of the mind, it is important to remember that you are not alone. There are many, many spirit Guides and teachers around you and they are here to assist you, but you must ask for their help. The universe may be one, but within this reality there are many laws, one of which is the law of non-interference.

With all requests of Spirit, I have always heard that I can ask that my energy fields be cleared with ease and grace. This request in my view equates to also asking for *no physical discomfort, please.* Just as a child who asks for growth, I have discovered that there is no guarantee that this expansion process will ever be pain free.

The next time you feel that you are experiencing the flu, a cold or possibly an overall body ache, ask yourself what you have been thinking and feeling that would cause you to feel this way. When I am in the midst of changing the way I think about a concept or have dishonored myself and gone against my inner knowing, my body usually reacts by causing the body to tense. The result of this may take form as lower intestinal issues, an ear ache, or a general pressure in my sinuses. If I become overly worried about some aspect of my life, I get a killer headache that may last for days until I finally understand how I need to shift my conscious awareness about the matter.

As you begin to incorporate life's awakenings into greater levels of awareness, just as a child learns that her horizon is beyond her own back yard, you too may equate your choices to your grand adventure.

There will always be times when you will want to retreat into the recesses of the mind by shutting down your heart. That is O.K. You are only respecting your human nature's desire for rest and safekeeping. At any given stage in your learning, you will consider just how steep the path of surrender will be. In doing so, realize that you are fully equipped to scale the peaks of enlightenment and always have been.

We cannot awaken to the soul's desire until we have surrendered our human nature to Spirit. As you practice this process of releasing fear-based beliefs, you will experience a wide-variety of phenomenon. By embracing the fragmented pieces of your soul, you may begin to feel like a caterpillar evolving into a butterfly. The process defies any logical or rational explanation, but you will recognize that this type of metamorphosis is taking place because of the physical sensations you are feeling.

As you begin to move through each new phase of change, you may sense energetic pressures or images of other worldly beings or smells that call you to suspend belief in fear long enough to surrender to the clearing process.

Once you are called to more fully surrender to Source, a feeling may come over you that will shake the very foundation of your most personal beliefs. Your outer world, once you have begun to shift inwardly, will also make a shift or change in circumstantial awakenings. These awakenings take the form of life happenings, relationship changes and in-depth remembrances of who you are.

The beginning stages of transformation are often prompted by upsets and re-organizations in your life and sometimes come with harrowing emotional changes. All and all it seems unavoidable. When God takes hold, the outer world must change to reflect the inner reality to connect more fully and open up new avenues for the soul's expression.

It cannot be stressed enough that during this time of change, you will transition at minimum, from stages of agitated emotionality and upheaval to a state of being that is more at peace. From the outside, because you have now surrendered to the greater will of God, your life is bound to feel transitional in nature, but from the inside you will know which direction you are headed. Allow peace to be your guide as you become the change you desire.

Each transitory cycle is unique. If your big issue is one of survival, your release of this fear may be to lose everything that stands in the way of recognizing who you are. Looking back at the example I used in chapter one, this was most certainly the case in my life. The deeper the fear, the harder the shake will be to get to the core of your illusions. When you invoke energetic shifting by calling forth the change you desire, your angels and guides are less concerned about comfort and more focused on getting the job done.

During these times, if you notice your heart beginning to open and your mind closing down the process, you could become very frustrated but just remember that this is a transitory part of your learning. You will think you are becoming resteeped in fear but you are not. As your energy fields begin to shift and realign themselves more fully with Source, you are releasing fear, not embracing it. However, if you begin to hold onto the emotions during this time by incessantly mulling over events or stewing over your decisions, your auric field will just take longer to clear and align with the new belief. Just remember when you feel the very emotion you have called forward for release, you are to first feel it to the fullest extent possible. It may at times feel overwhelming but that is O.K. Embrace the feeling and recognize that it is a part of you that is ready to be transmuted into a higher expression of who you are. It is merely a belief that is no longer serving you. Let it go. Let it all go.

As you move through the release process consider these few guidelines as you begin to experience a variety of phenomena:

1. Pay close attention to the emotion as it prompts you to release and transform the lower energetic thought form attached to it into a higher expression of love.

2. Remember to embrace *all* fragments of your soul that call out for change. You will first experience this as self-

134

hate and –loathing. No one feels this but you. You may have buried this feeling so deep within you that you are in total denial of this quality of your inner self.

This is where actively forgiving yourself comes into play. By the very nature of recognizing these soul fragments you are calling back the greater part of your soul. You are not only healing the lower personality and raising your quality of life but you are discerning the part you played in your own undoing. This serves the purpose to solidify the learning as you gather yet finer pieces of your soul and energetically transmute any and all vibrational frequencies that are no longer in full alignment with your soul's highest expression.

To aid in this self-discovery process, ask your angels and Guides to provide you with an image or sign that will ignite your imagination. Then wait a period of 48 hours. Normally an awakening occurs within this time before the personality jumps in to kill the imagery or stifle the feeling with cynicism.

An illustration of this type of asking can be seen in the following story shared with me by a friend. A beautiful young woman asked her guides to give her a clear message that would explain why she was not meeting the husband of her dreams. The very next day, she received a call from a man who asked her for a dinner date. She quickly learned that he was married. Learning this, she immediately realized that Spirit was giving her the answer she was seeking. No matter how beautiful, smart or well dressed she was, energetically she was broadcasting a message that she was emotionally unavailable.This revelation opened the door to clear the energetic block that was holding her away from realizing her heart's desire.

Once you have recognized the answer to your question write it down, draw yourself a picture or do something like a dance, a shout or *any* expression of joy to remind yourself before the mind suppresses the feeling of expansion.

The purpose of resonating with your highest expression is to bring your energy fields into full alignment with the actions you will take. Remember to check in from time to time and ask yourself what inspires your imagination. Depending on your resolve to follow your heart, this feeling within you will change and take on different but similar permutations of the same vibratory pattern. When it does, keep reminding yourself of your divine nature. During times of great change and energetic shifting, just remember to re-align your thoughts with that of a creator in charge of your creations as you continue to follow your inner guidance.

As you begin actively calling forth your higher Light and begin shifting in consciousness, your physical body is bound to feel the affects of God's grace. We receive this energetic awakening from Spirit through the meridians that run throughout the physical vessel. If you were to look at a map of the human body showing the meridians, you would see millions of energy zones running vertically from your head to the tips of your fingers and the end of your toes. In the center following the line along your spine, are vortexes of energy called chakras that act as main transmitters and trans-ducers for the body's electrical system. They also act as connecting points between your left and right sides and as the internal channel for connecting you to the grid system.

As you receive the higher frequencies of Light, the energy runs through your system from head to toe, toe to head. If your energy bodies are clear of emotional debris, the energy flows freely. If there are blockages, the clearing may take on a life all its own. Just remember that it is a process and be patient with yourself.

With incoming energy, your auric field absorbs the higher frequency as your body pushes out the lower debris that you have called to release. You put this process into motion by stating your intent to transmute all lower expressions of your divine self for realizing your soul's highest expression. This pushing out of the *old* will call up painful memories or may push you to *react* to situations in old patterned ways. However, as you focus on your clearing process, the shift in energy will push you to clear all lower emotions, beliefs and circumstances that no longer support your newly stated intention.

God may grant you grace in the form of this type of energetic awakening, but if you are to sustain the higher frequencies of Light, your permanent release of old patterns is what allows the higher vibration to begin assimilating into the physical. This is accomplished by surrendering to the clearing process that you first invoked. As you are prompted to do so, release whatever emotional, mental or physical block comes up as a result of this. Clear it from your energy bodies by embracing your awakening.

It will be quite obvious when you have completed the process because you will no longer feel dazed or disoriented by the particular set of circumstances that have just arisen and have reached a high state of joy as you fully acknowledge and appreciate the 'aha' moment that arises from taking affirmative action.

Remembering that everything within us and in our world is dynamically, movable energy, this concept makes the saying 'what goes around comes around' a literal statement. The energy of transformation, fueled by your intent, gains momentum through your actions, and by doing what brings you joy, you will quickly transform your life.

12. Learn to identify secondary desires

As you remember the source of your creation and take the action that is in alignment with your heart's desire, your whole world will begin to open up. However, as it does, it may do so in seemingly unfamiliar and less than optimal circumstances. This is because you may manifest, as you begin the clearing process, secondary desires.

A secondary desire is created when you have stated your intent to manifest your soul's highest expression, then a belief or doubt creeps into your consciousness. This quickly produces a situation or circumstance that closely mirrors your heart's desire, but instead creates pain and hardship, or a general feeling of having achieved something less than your intended outcome.

For instance, your heart's desire may be to realize your freedom but the secondary may say, "but only if I am smart enough, kind enough, good enough," etc. This *only if* causes a secondary set of circumstances to appear. In this instant, you are unaware of the secondary desire as you have set your intent into motion but manifest much less than your desired outcome.

Now, this is not to say that all secondary desires are not valid. They are. It must also be said that the manifestation of a secondary desire is often times a signal that a fear belief is hidden somewhere in your psyche that you have yet to recognize. Therefore, this belief has blocked you from the higher vibration of realizing your highest expression.

It is important to discover these secondaries and the beliefs that create them. This can occur by doing the following:

1. Ask your higher self, "What is the belief that is blocking me from realizing my highest expression?" After you have asked the question, put it out of your mind and trust that your answer will come. Your guidance may be given in a dream, a situation or simply and most profoundly as a deep inner knowing. If your mind is busy on the search, you are not open to hear. The key is to ask, then to be still as you trust the process.

2. Remember who you are. You are a divine creator and have commanded a secondary out of your own blindness. Embrace this part of your creation and know that you have honored your belief. You are also acknowledging that you no longer need this belief because you now remember who you are.

Secondary desires are produced from fear beliefs because you subconsciously expect failure. Know that there is no fear in your heart's desire. If you find an element of doubt in a secondary, then you are to release it as you embrace your divinity.

This sounds as simple as saying the words and feeling the effect of your effort, but you are also a human being rooted in your physical surroundings. Before you can fully manifest your heart's desire, you must release all secondary outcomes. The degree of emotion you process as you release will depend upon how 'rooted' you are in old beliefs that no longer serve you.

It cannot be said that one God is greater than another. We are all great God beings of Light who have come to realize how love calls forth pain and anguish to dissolve before our very eyes.

Secondaries come in all forms and sometimes will cause you great angst as you navigate through life. Your human nature sometimes, and in spite of yourself, will get the better part of you and push you into a state of confusion.

When this happens, it is necessary to remember the source of your creation. Many times we can move through life at such a fast clip that we forget to take the time to get quiet or to reconnect with the higher part of ourselves.

This disconnection occurs when you are so much in the flow of life that you become that greater part of the vastness, then you forget and the ego slips in. You have slowly gotten off track and before you know it you are in the lost thatch of a thick forest and cannot seem to get out.

When you feel you are lost, you may also feel betrayed by someone or something that has *put you there*. In actuality you have just forgotten to check in with Source along the way. It is because you slowly but surely allowed your ego to slip in and tell you how great you were in such a way as to break your very connection with the greater part of yourself.

You may see this in others but rarely do we see it in ourselves until we have found ourselves in the wasteland of doubt and self-pity. After you have fully recognized this state of mind as misaligned with the feeling you have when you are in Source, the feeling of joy and peace, you can then look back and see exactly where you got off track. This kind of looking back or assessing has nothing to do with the events of what happened but everything to do with how you are feeling about yourself.

It is as if Spirit operates best with the *outer* view of the world covered so that only the *inner* view of life can be discerned. Our navigational system and connection with Source most certainly resides deep within the recesses of the heart and the only way to access that inner beacon of Light is by listening; first and foremost. Sometimes we are so embittered; this is very hard to do. During these times, it is important to become recentered.

The tools to do so may be as simple as taking a few deep breaths to get yourself back on balance, spending time in nature by taking a walk or finding a quiet spot that overlooks a beautiful valley, river or the quiet of your own backyard. Listening to meditative or classically inspired music is a calming agent and elevates your vibration. Carrying a favorite pendant or something that reminds you of who you are is also helpful.

13. Enjoy the learning as you join with others who are also working to release old patterns of behavior

You may find the most powerful allies for keeping on task is the camaraderie and encouragement of one another. There is no secondary in deep spiritually centered friendships. The learning curve is steep for those who take that big leap into the void of understanding. Once you do, you will find others right behind you and in front, who have also taken that same leap into the void and are relishing the thrill of this new way of learning.

When you realize that others too transgress into fear, you may realize that you are not alone. By the same token, when you see others manifesting their visions, then you too may be encouraged and deeply grateful to be in the presence of love united with Spirit.

This is not to say that there is a continuum of learning in the sense of levels and layers like fields of study. You are here with others as one mind, one heart and one body of collective knowledge.

In spiritually centered camaraderie, the joy is mutually shared. When one *gets it,* everyone gets it. This is the way of learning. It is most exciting and downright exhilarating to learn life's most astounding lessons of the heart in the midst of others who are also on the path of transformation.

When the sages and mystics of old tell their stories through the many ways of reenactment such as storytelling and dance, we marvel at their wisdom and wonder. Our forebears knew the secrets of the universe and we are left to discover the trail like Sherlock Holmes solving the greater mystery. As with any good mystery, the solution is usually right under our very noses.

It is the same with matters of the heart. If you can set aside your fear of failure, then you are half way home. The other half merely requires that you honor yourself as you honor others and remember the source of your creation.

It is never enough to say, "It is all in God's hands." This saying is an honorable one if meant in the way it was given to us. Unfortunately down through time the greater part of humanity has become convinced that God is out there somewhere, not inside within the inner sanctum of the heart.

You can say, "Oh but I know this is true. God *is* within me. I take orders from no one but me, the higher part of me." I challenge you to consider the nuances between surrendering to God and surrendering to the God within.

As you refine your listening patterns, it is important to affirm who you are as a part of your daily prayer routine. It is also important to be totally free from any self-judgment or chastisement of self. This is a tall order considering that most of us are our own worst enemy. What moves through many a mind is nothing compared to what the personality self moves into consciousness.

This way of changing your consciousness, though, is detached from the mindful intentions of self-driven perfection.

I say perfection because many who leap into the void of their own understanding may first surrender out of fear but later become extremely reliant on their faith in God. Your orientation to your faith has carried you thus far. It is a positive developmental cycle and one that requires a great amount of self-discipline. However, your soul will eventually push you into an identification crisis to clear even your misalignment with your belief in God.

This push is designed to take you into a deeper state of surrender. You are likely to experience it much in the same way as the first cathartic release that took your spiritual awakening by storm. As you move through yet another more disturbing career change, health scare or change in your relationships or the need to change your environment, don't be surprised if you experience self-loathing as you muster the courage to trust this deeper call to release and rebuild the self. As you shed beliefs that are closer to your very identification with God, you are likely to feel disoriented, angry and out of control at times, but simply affirm your path, let go and trust.

My life took another turn very recently as my soul decided it was time for me to more deeply surrender to path and purpose. While totally focused on forging ahead with River of Light Enterprise, the organization I founded after leaving my job of over eight years, I quietly felt the inner push to begin the writing that my guides kept telling me about. For months, I kept hearing, during my daily meditations, that I was 'to walk away from the river and to trust, simply trust.' The fact of the matter is that I understood the words but not the full meaning of the guidance; I was just not *getting it*. After much soul searching and prompting from those closest to me, I finally identified the secondary desire and released it.

My guides were asking me to relinquish the *river* of doubt and indecision that I had been holding onto, and to write; just write. This past year of doing just that provided me the space to dive deeper than I could have ever imagined into my relationship with those who guide me. This time of writing also gave me the encouragement and sense of safety to begin to more fully trust my inner guidance.

Even after having gone through many evolutions of your own way of releasing fear since that first time, you may begin to resist the transformational cycles at work. The personality part of yourself will sometimes rear its head and begin to push a secondary forward instead. When this occurs you may likely be saying to yourself, "I'm O.K. here and I'm very happy. There is no need to move out of complacency. I am at the highest vibratory pattern that is needed right now. I wish to go no further."

Like the example I just gave, your soul may have been sending you the signal to change but your higher mind was resisting or holding steady and keeping this prompting from you out of fear. On the personality level, you may actually be discerning that all is well. As this resistance to change is occurring, you will likely feel happy, content and in the flow. You may see no reason to change or to check in with Source.

These are the times when you may have been checking in but, in retrospect, find that only a part of your inner heart was being totally honest with yourself. At this point, there was a part of you that truthfully did not want to hear that you were being called to change and grow, or to shed what was no longer serving you. In truth you are always in the flux and flow of change.

You may wish to switch this part of yourself into auto flow or may wish to revisit this fact at will. Regardless of your method of flowing with your highest expression for fulfilling your desire to transform your fears, know that you will always be called to change. That is the one thing about life that is constant—that life is always changing as our soul pushes us to grow.

After you have gone through the initial stage of birthing into the newness of life you will begin discerning what is best and right for yourself differently.

As you do, two questions will consistently come up:

1. "Am I on the path for the highest expression of my heart's desire and the good of all concerned?"

2. "Have I fully surrendered in fulfillment of my heart's desire?"

These are valid questions and once answered, will take you into a state of joyful gladness and clear the way to actualize your heart's desire. It is only by perpetually surrendering your fears to God that you will hear this inner prompting. And just remember, what is right for another may not be right and best for you. The way you choose to learn is strictly personal and you are to custom design the vibratory patterns that best fit your soul's most wondrous journey.

ASKING ABOUT THE PHYSICAL SHAPING OF LIFE

This is a sample of the many answers that took form for the purpose of pointing me in a different direction.

More than money, more than words, many questions remain unanswered. How, what, when, tonight, tomorrow, today…

Sai: How many souls ask these questions daily, weekly, hourly and minute by minute?

How many souls ask about trust and reconciliation, about love and peace? All want answers to trivial questions without asking for the answers that bring about harmony.

The key component to peace is love. Love conquers all. Love is all. It is with your heart centered on the love of God, love of heart, love of all that one's heart and mind will quiet of trivial pursuits. The game of learning was invented for fun.

And so is life. Life is fun.

Do not take the seriousness of the world to heart. 'Love all, serve all' is a simple statement to keep within your heart to balance your endeavors with perspective.

It is with reverence that we beseech you to tone your heart and mind to matters that remain at the center of peace and harmony. Do not succumb to petty matters.

Love. Light. Honor your soul force.

Honor others by your undying love of others. Reflect back to them what they cannot see for themselves. Honor your mother. Honor your father. All is well.

—July 27, 1996

LEAPING INTO THE VOID

Guides: You have leapt into the void.
You must now trust in its outcome.

All is well my child.

I am confused.

Guides: Christ is within all of us. Each soul has made
a choice, upon which they must follow their path. It has
been set up this way from the millennium. You must
always trust that all is well.
You are always to know that the best will come to all
who ask.

Each soul has a separate path and yet we are all the
same.

You must hold strong to your belief.
Everything that you have been taught does not isolate
you but unites you with the oneness.

What you are feeling is the separation from humanity.
You must step, must come to the other side.
You continually want to straddle the physical.
This will cause you great pain as you are
 experiencing it now.

You must release your worry, your doubts, your
sadness and know that all is well.

You are loved beyond all comprehension.
What awaits you is the glory within.
Release and behold the glory within.

We are with you and you with us.
We are one.
Rejoice.
And have faith.

—April 15, 1992

Overcoming Resistance to Change

Why do I want to retreat?

Guides: You are at the pinnacle of leaping into the void and you are scared.

You are afraid that if you allow your soul to merge with the Divine that you will lose all that is you, that what you identify with will be lost to the forces within.

Do not be afraid.

You are to trust your inner knowing.
You know you will be safe.

You are to trust what we are giving you.
Your emotions are resisting the change.
Do not allow yourself to be overcome by old conditioning.

There is no longer any need.
Harm will not come to you.
You have nothing to be afraid of.
He will not hurt you. We will not allow it.
It is not to be....

You are truly blessed.
This is a time of rejoicing.
Know that this is so and give thanks.

Do not allow the worldly order to scare you.
There is nothing that can stand in the way.
Nothing will harm you. You have only to open yourself up and to trust in all that is being given to you is for your protection and growth.

You have paid your dues. The penalty for your spiritual freedom has been great but know that you are now free.

Rejoice. This is a time for great expansion and learning for you.

Be patient, be kind and know that you are progressing toward a divine union.

All is well.
Rejoice.
Rejoice, Rejoice.
All is well.

And give thanks to God.

—February 2, 1992

Too many steps have been
Taken returning to the root
And the source.
Better to have been blind
And deaf from the beginning!
Dwelling in one's true abode,
Unconcerned with that without—
The river flows tranquilly
On and the flowers are red.

—Kakuan (1100-1200)

CHAPTER FIVE

VIBRATIONAL SHIFTING

Making the choice to shake off the last vestiges of delusional thinking may cause the body to shake and quiver but it is a small price to pay for the expansive feeling of liberation at hand.

Adjusting to change that you are becoming

Many truth seekers realize they are not alone in their quest to realize their highest expression of who they are. These are the individuals who relish in the learning. They can be identified by their open determination to do and to be a beacon of Light.

It is not uncommon to encounter many souls on a single pass up the mountain of joy. The journey off the beaten path can most certainly be challenging, but it is also exhilarating. For me, there is one adventure that still brings a strong remembrance of much laughter and silliness to mind. Several years ago, I was asked by a friend to accompany her and another friend to go see a man who runs a retreat center. He is a very wise, incredibly gifted soul who teaches the stuff of transformation in ways that allow for perfect unfolding, yet in unpredictable self-discovery ways. I arrived with the singular expectation of being a support for my friend.

The weekend started by our host asking each of us what we had come for. When it came time for me to answer his question of, "Why are you here?" The conversation quickly turned to, why I was here for *me*. As he probed into why I had *really* come, our conversation turned to faith. Little did I know that my faith was about to be tested, but in the most surreal yet outrageously funny, scary, thought-provoking ways imaginable. All learning aside, as I look back, the feeling I am left with is pure, unadulterated joyousness. I realize now that the actual lesson I had come to experience was how life is to be lived in the moment and letting go of all expectations is key to feeling that sense of joy and adventure. This is where the real test of my faith will be realized—by learning to become this vibration in all areas of my life, not just desiring it to be so.

At some point in time, after you have taken that leap of faith, you will wake up one morning or realize in the midst of an activity or conversation that you are no longer fearful.

It is a strange sensation on one level because, at least for me anyway, fear has been such an integral part of my life. For something so elemental to fall deep into the background of my life was pretty profound. Fear can and still does cause an emotional spike as I encounter the challenges of my learning. That is normal. I realize now, that we are not meant to be super human, but what I am addressing, is the day-to-day vibratory patterns as I move through life.

Just remember that everyone gets scared and that is O.K. There are no rules outside the Law of Oneness (divine love in action), which transcends all other universal principles.

However, we are never without our learning curve. It is always present and forever more egging us on. As learning becomes the constant, your own unique way of seeing and building confidence for taking action will continue to be challenged. Your Guides will always challenge you to transcend your fears. As you act courageously by taking the steps that are laid before you, you will find that it gets easier to discern 'highest' and 'greatest' choice when you are in the still point of the moment.

Affirmations serve valuable intonations in reaffirming your resonance with God essence.

You will spend a lot of time discovering how to move through the stages of your learning but the prompting to change will, at first, come with the onset of impending inner turmoil. When you feel a general sense of uneasiness come over you, move through this simple two step process.

1. As you invoke the change, remind yourself of who you are by repeating the statement "I am that I am. I am God incarnate in physicality." By doing so you will reset the mind and put the heart in charge.

2. Then say, "I surrender fully and completely to the greater will of the Divine that I am."

You may already be seeking to transcend the cycle of fear that has shaped your life to date and are learning to step differently in the world. We, who actively direct our lives by working from this place of peace, are growing in numbers every day. As you work to clear away the heavy emotions, you will find that it is not an easy task, but one that brings great joy as you shed each outer covering that no longer serves you.

As you do so, keep surrendering your fears to God for realizing your highest expression. This allows the mind to sit idle while the soul speaks unfiltered bypassing long held beliefs. Of course, some will say that it is not possible to hear from Source without a filter. A filter is an emotional/mental blind spot that blocks or distorts our perception of what we are hearing. We each live our lives through filters because it is the way the soul sets the stage for growth. As you peel these layers of filters away, your doubt about listening to your heart will also melt away.

As you intend that God reveal your highest expression to you, prepare to receive your answer. It may come as a huge surprise to learn that your primary purpose is to learn to love more fully, completely and unconditionally. Whatever expression your heart's desire takes to learn that is O.K. You are here for the soul's journey and it has nothing to do with who you are or where you have come from. It has only to do with what choices you have made along the way and what choice you make from this point forward.

At some point you may ask, "How can I make a difference?" The answer can be found in the transcendence of worldly pursuits and formulated in the higher expressions of love. You will only be able to sustain it by continuing to raise your vibration. This level of sustainability in numbers is what positively impacts whole systems of governance and world populations.

It takes courage to put your faith in God as you follow your intuition. Taking the inner view that comes from Source and expressing it outwardly calls for courage of a different kind. This is not the self-actualizing courage you may remember as you think about competing sports teams or foot soldiers and armies of opposing forces, for instance. There are no opponents in these acts of courageousness, only right action.

This type of action is divinely inspired for the expression of altruism and for no other reason. You may be called to perform myriad acts of kindness or heroism unseen, and unannounced. There is no fanfare, awards banquets or press releases celebrating your efforts, but Spirit rewards these acts of selflessness. You will find that when Spirit reciprocates, your life changes in ways far more awesome than any outward show of thanks from those you helped.

Kindness of heart is not a worldly commodity but is a foundational way of operating in the world, it is the way one spiritual being recognizes the other.

Even without engaging in the giving that is prompted when the heart is fully open, there are many ways your heart can be opened even when not consciously choosing to transform. For instance you may do community service for the sake of earning a greater degree of social standing or to build a resume to get a better job. You may start out with an ulterior motive but if your heart is opened in the process, that is all that matters. It leads the way for another way of being in the world. This unconscious approach to spiritual awakening is an honorable way of transforming the most hardened heart center.

It is the same with our world leaders today. As we watch them make choices that reflect the current state of mass consciousness, it is obvious that many are out of touch with the spiritual law of oneness. They are to take big steps, but to do so with little regard to spiritual law, spirals whole regions of people down into the emotional pit of despair. Though the great Roman society claimed many a victory and land for their own, they eventually perished from their own corruption and sadistic debauchery. Will we go the same road? Not if we can grow out of the ruins of humanity and shift the paradigm. On the surface of life, given our penchant for aggression, it would seem that the current path of humanity is to perish. Each choice leads to a path of learning. We will always have the choice to change our present reality, as well as our future.

We are all leaders in the new world consciousness that is coming. We have only to find our way by listening to the prompting of the higher power that leads us to our heart's desire. There is never to be a qualification of right or best for another. You are in charge of your own individual path of spiritual evolvement. Only you know what is best for yourself. I cannot judge another just as you cannot judge me. I have come to think of it as a matter of perspective. As you move to clear fear from your energy bodies and progress into the higher states of consciousness, it will become more and more obvious that the more we think we know, the less we really do.

The mind is like that, always searching and the only way it has for settling on something is to compare it with or against something else. Our human nature is forever striving for the best by knocking the other. As soon as you realize you are comparing yourself to someone or even against your own expectations, drop the internal dialog and affirm that you are free of such constraints.

We live in the world of mixed emotions, and it is very difficult not to be swept into the halls of comparable condemnation. When you find yourself engaged in a conversation or an environment that is dwelling on this kind of interchange, your energy centers will signal to you when it is time to depart because your physical discomfort will rise above what is tolerable.

Hatred for another comes with a heavy price to pay. In reality, all hate is directed at the self. When you find yourself in the midst of projecting a lower emotion onto someone or become the target of another's projection, simply walk away or transmute it to a higher plane of consciousness. You can consciously change the exchange of energy by more fully connecting with Source while still engaged with others. To do so, turn your thoughts to kindness and appreciation for the God within. This active form of acceptance of another, if practiced, becomes a natural part of your day-to-day interactions.

This feeling of being in Source is unmistakable. You cannot force it nor will it to be so. It is a natural state of being. Once you have become practiced at being there often—every day, moment to moment—you will find it much easier to reside there in times of stress.

Once you are in this state, the lower forms of expression can no longer continue. The higher vibration of acceptance overtakes the lower to such an extent that speaking and feeling in the lower states will melt into a space of quiet peacefulness and settle into a calmer way of relating to one another. As you become accustomed to and practiced at this level of feeling, you will sense lower thought wave patterns in others and avoid them altogether.

Where there is peace, fear cannot be. Love transcends all fear. However, we, as divine beings have forgotten this basic piece of knowledge and continually surrender our Light to another time and time again. With practice you will learn to identify with love and seek out those who resonate at this same frequency of life-affirming behavior.

As you awaken to the higher realms of understanding you are reminded that only God knows all, sees all. You have studied and worked hard to arrive at this place in time. You may look around and recognize the many family members around you. They may not be your birth brothers and sisters, but you will recognize them by their inner Light.

After you have made your own leap into the void of understanding, you will look back and remember the many souls who have surrounded you with their own brand of awakenings and will begin to appreciate how they have helped you grow. It is because of their grand adventure into the unknown that you draw courage to accept what is before you with ease and grace. At a time when there are seemingly no rules outside of the beacon of love that burns so brightly within you, this assurance will propel you deeper into your quest to realize your freedom.

You grant your fellow travelers adieu and wish them God's speed, grace and enlightenment. It is scary stuff to leave the safety of secure, safe, predictable relationships and orientations to life. Who would want to?

I am reminded that we are all explorers every day. There comes a time when motivation becomes motion. It takes courage to launch into the unknown but that is how great discoveries are made.

Shifting from one vibration into another is easy in Spirit terms, but we as spiritual beings reside in the *real* world of dense matter. It is the mental, physical and etheric fields that give humankind pause because we are so used to relying on such a limited way of being. The filters we have created by the beliefs we hold onto create a world that is full of contradictions, yet we hold onto the old at all costs and shoot down the other who sees differently.

Spirit says go, the higher mind says, 'Wait a minute," or "let's talk about that," or simply, "no, not in this lifetime." Many individuals on the personality level say "yes" to the prompting of Spirit, only to witness the higher mind say "no."

One example of this is a person who acknowledges his desire to change some aspect of his life. He opens his heart to God and affirms his intention to transform his lower feelings of fear into a higher level of consciousness. His soul is calling him to change, but his higher mind, the part of him that has stored culminated life lessons and kept track of all the fear-laden lessons, discerns whether it is safe to do so. On the personality level, he may not understand why things are happening to him, but the higher mind is well aware. At this point, the goal of the personality self is to bypass the higher mind and more fully identify with the soul.

With the many repetitions of holding onto hurt and pain as a part of our learning, we take more stock in the higher mind. The higher mind is not the intellect, the ego or the subconscious. It is the lower vibrational part of the soul that knows a bigger part of the picture, but not the soul's life journey. It discerns what to trust, and what and how much change to accept. The purpose for its existence is rooted in survival and to help fine-tune our alignment with Source.

The personality self is the thinker/doer while the higher mind is the moderator of the lessons, and, of course, the soul knows the whole story. This is the simplified version and one that may serve as a backdrop to your learning.

If you choose to actively engage the mind in clearing these blockages, you will need to intend that a clear channel be established between you and your soul. I speak to this concept of the *self* in plurality, but in actuality we are one continuous column of Light.

There is no set way for clearing energy fields. You may find this process most difficult at times and at others, it will

159

serve as a time-tested potion for almost hysterical laughter, silliness, and joy at every turn. As you clear and release lower emotions and beliefs from your auric field, you may experience mood swings from melancholy to optimism and unexplainable physical ailments.

You can clear these blockages by diving deeply into the emotions, though it does not have to be this way. It can also be done by simply recognizing your learning and releasing the belief that is holding you in fear.

As I witness the individuals who have shifted from fear to joy, it is a sight I will never forget. These are the times when a person who has been struggling to understand what is before them and has come to a crossroads in life. When they realize their learning, in the instant of their revelation, a quickening of Spirit occurs. It is as if a little piece of heaven descends upon them and their auric field implodes with an energetic burst igniting a bright, radiant Light. This energetic burst of joy is at first profusely white, then quickly turns to a soft glow as the person relaxes into their knowing. The sight is profoundly beautiful because of the love embued within it.

During these first few moments of Spirit bursting forth, there are many angelic beings from the ethereal realms on hand to witness the event as if to say, "We are here with you and rejoicing in your self-discovery." It is hard to imagine the world without them.

Angelic beings are here to help and guide us to our highest potential as we seek to merge with the greater part of ourselves. We are all there is. We are everything and everywhere. There is no need for protection if we are experiencing full unadulterated joy, love and peace. There are times when we are afraid or doubtful. These are the times when we open ourselves up to the Divine in a feeling that is needy. In our time of need, if our intent is not purely aligned with our highest expression, we will inadvertently invite lower octaves of Light into our auric field.

During this stage of your learning, it takes time to discern, for instance, between a disincarnate soul and an angelic being. They can look and feel the same at first. I have since discovered that, energetically, any Light being who tells me what to do or creates a qualifier by making me feel that I am anything less than unconditionally loved, is confused and merely reflecting back to me my own state of confusion.

When I am in meditation, my mind is always focused on the God within as I affirm my highest expression. As I do so, I sense the many angelic beings around me. Over time, I have also become more aware of the beings who are pushing into my energy field trying to experience life in the physical. Now that I understand this dynamic, I do not allow it.

In popular terms, disincarnate souls have been called demons or ghosts. They are actually disincarnate entities or souls that are lower vibrational fragments of humanity's own manifestations. I have experienced ghost-like entities in homes and many in the community where I reside. One such time occurred when I was waiting for a colleague to come over to help me with a River of Light project.

Just before he arrived, I walked across the main hallway only to come face to face with a tall, darkly handsome, Union civil war officer dressed in long coat tails with dark hair and full beard. He stood in my living room staring, one foot in front of the other, looking back at me. My first reaction was fear, then as quickly as I registered the emotion, I dismissed it. As I stared back at him, I blessed him as I more fully connected with the Divine. He quickly faded and I went on about my business.

When my colleague arrived, I told him what had happened, then went upstairs to work on my computer. As I was working, my attention turned to the hallway where I watched as a confederate soldier with hat and long bayonet walked down the hallway away from me. Once again, I felt a spike of fear, then quickly dismissed it as I connected to Source with blessings to this soul.

I was reminded that when I first moved to this home, I was asked to pray for the soldiers on the hill who were still trapped in their confusion. During that time, I lived in an area where some of the most bitter, prolonged battles of the Civil war were fought. This experience preceded many strange encounters with the fragments of other souls who were also trapped in altered realities and resided in a confused state of being.

If you feel you are experiencing a depressed state or feel out of sorts, just affirm your highest vibration and claim your birthright—that you are a child of God and accept only that which is for your highest good. When you are opening yourself up to Source, pay close attention to how you are feeling. Accept no qualifiers. You will know this feeling as you cast off the nuances of fear. If you are sensing anything less than perfect joy and oneness, then you know you have encountered an energy or force that is weighing you down or trying to gain entry into your auric field. When this occurs, bless the soul by first acknowledging the feeling, then intend that you are embracing any fragmented parts of yourself as you transmute any lower frequencies to your highest expression of love. Intend also that anything less than your highest good leave your auric field now.

We are truly one and there is only a thin veil that separates us from the etheric beings who are experiencing life energetically. Our experience in the body is unique because we have the privilege of physically *rooting* our spirits in the earth's vibration. This act of rooting is accomplished by first making the choice to be here, then consciously choosing to live joyfully.

Just as we are transforming, the earth is also preparing itself for a shift. At some point, the earth will experience a quickening during a time when the larger percentage of humanity will be in resonance and harmony with the earth's vibrational frequency. We must remember that we are not only souls traveling through what we perceive as time and space, we are space travelers within galaxies of Light.

As we make the shift from fear to love, we are reminded that all worlds are of one Light. We are all one because we are united in the feeling of love. The higher vibratory patterns come as no surprise to humankind, yet we sometimes move through our world with the basic animal instincts of a tiger. The tiger is not an aggressive animal unless it is hungry or provoked. However, once it is either, it becomes aggressive and powerful in its pursuit of prey. Like the tiger, humanity has learned to remember the source of our creation, but we have forgotten the true meaning of our remembrance—that we are a single race of people.

As you continue to raise your vibration, you will begin to discover the many images and memories of other times, other worlds. As you witness the part you played in humanity's evolutionary journey, keep an open mind and decide to be O.K. with whatever comes up. Simply bless and release it all without going too far into an inner questing period. By doing so, it will free your mind so that even more images will come up for release. It is important to allow this process to take place, because these impressions are a part of what is creating the blockages in your energy fields. I am speaking to the many sensations and remembrances of your time on earth and seemingly in other realities and other dimensions. Because it is a fascinating part of humanity's journey, you can easily get stuck trying to figure out or hold onto those memories as your prize possessions. These are all aspects of yourself that are calling you to release the lower vibrations of the learning you are still holding onto, and to embrace all that you are.

The core feeling of being separated from God comes from these memory fragments that have taken form as altered states of reality. In some cases they have become alter egos of your personality. When this stronger fragmentation occurs, the ego takes on another identity and pushes at your mind's will to survive.

It may take an act of faith to render this part of yourself whole again but when you do, you will feel very thankful for having been led astray. Only then will you realize there was an incredible amount of learning that took place while a part of your soul was in this separated state.

This phenomenon is like bringing two twins into the world. Rather than separating them into different bedrooms, they are separated into two different families. Once brought back together and reconnected emotionally, they find the plethora of their individual experiences have not only enriched their bond but also strengthened their collective knowledge base.

There may be a part of you that wishes to remain fragmented for the sake of learning, but your stronger desire now is to bring the pieces of your higher consciousness back into full alignment with Source.

I have been working on this process for a few years now. I first became aware of it in late 1998 after experiencing a force of energy that was so intense, it caused my head to shake violently as the energy shot through my system while in deep meditation. It was painful and frustrating to say the least. I surrendered to what was happening because, at the time, I felt I was resisting some kind of transformation that was beyond my immediate understanding.

I asked many, many questions about the source of what I was experiencing and received the answer in the form of visual and spoken communication. I came to the understanding that there was a vast part of my soul that was still in a higher realm of learning but that this higher part of my soul was being called back to Source.

There seemed to be nothing I could do about the shaking but to accept, be patient and try to understood. While my guides worked on clearing major energy blockages in the body, I was guided to explore other dimensions, other realms. As I did so, I experienced varied altered states of reality, other worlds.

Over the past couple of years, as I have continued to surrender to the clearing process, the shaking has become less and less violent to the point that it is very mild compared to what it used to be. I still feel energy in my body this way but without the blockages. The energetic streaming feels like a fast rush of energy pushing through the top of my head and pulsing down through the core of me at such a fast clip, the feeling sometimes takes my breath away. I have learned to quickly move into a neutral state of awareness as I witness this phenomenon without judgment. As I continue to practice this state of being, I am able to access vast layers of knowledge that I have yet to fully understand, but trust that full knowing will come when I am ready.

As you move through your own way of clearing energetic blocks, and we all have them, just trust whatever process of release your higher self sets into motion and be patient with yourself enough to see it through.

Looking back, the writings I had been receiving were preparing me for this kind of transition long before I realized what was coming. My guides began telling me about a new mission for several years before I transitioned into this more Spirit-guided way of living.

After working a highly stressful, politically volatile project, I was suddenly set free. With less day-to-day pressure, this kind of physical shifting only intensified and forced me to fully focus inwardly. With this increased inner exploration of the self came an expanded state of awareness. During these past five years, there were times that I thought I would never come out of it and fully regain my earthly bearings.

This past year, as I began to honor my heart's desire of writing and speaking about what I intuitively know, the insistent voices of my inner guidance calmed and my vision that saw more Spirit than physical has begun to return to a *normal* state. Speaking of normal, my definition of normal has changed dramatically. The more I listen to my intuition, the more I feel the universe supporting me.

Having just come out of the most intense period of this learning, I encourage you to seek out answers by getting quiet and ask God to lead the way. Your soul knows what your higher

166

purpose is and what you have intended prior to this particular incarnation, but it is up to you here, now, to affirm your heart's desire and keep affirming it until your energy fields have cleared.

Bringing your heart into alignment with Source increases the energetic exchange with the soul. As you shift away from the nuances of fear into the higher states of love, your auric field will change with every subtle thought. Just keep calling forward, for release, all that is holding you back. As you do so, you will remember and you will forget as you move through the many stages of the emotional shattering of the self. Seek to remember your divine nature as you learn more about your soul, even while in a filtered state of amnesia. If you begin to feel yourself losing sight of your ultimate goal, get quiet and affirm who you are.

It is very difficult to remember who you are when you are forever inundated with sights and sounds that tell you otherwise; but that is where the heart of the matter meets all passways into the soul. It is your soul's desire to be free from strife, doubt and indecision. On one hand, after you are immersed in change, your higher mind may still be immobilized by the inertia required to shift from a state of being that is neutral or protective to one that is proactively engaged in and communicates with the personality self.

The personality part of your soul continues to enjoy life by stepping into greater awareness as you seek out answers to life's questions. This is a vital part of the process, but one that becomes encumbered when the mind discerns, through the filters of hard learning, that the new energy the soul is introducing is a threat to its very survival. The goal, in this human experience, is to clear all energetic blockages.

So the question begs to be answered; How do you clear the more subtle blockages? And how do you recognize when you are speaking to the higher mind and when you are connecting directly to your soul?

The answer for clearing the nuances of these more subtle energetic blocks can be found only when you are in the still point of your creation. This can be very tricky to discern at first because the personality part of your soul is very enmeshed in the physical reality of life. The difference in feeling between the higher mind and the soul is that your soul has no qualifiers. A qualifier is any sense of constraint when in the open state of readiness to receive guidance from the higher self.

While in the still point state of being, if you discern that you have accessed Source, but you are also sensing a qualifier to this feeling of ecstasy and expansiveness, then you are not in Source. You are in the thick of the higher mind and can go no further without clearing the lower vibrational debris that is blocking you from fully realizing your freedom.

The greater part of your soul will always call out for change. This is the part that is totally in balance and eternally peaceful with all that you are. In human terms you may interpret this as 'doing' something, but in reality clearing the illusions of the higher mind occurs within the stillness of your heart.

It is not necessary to belabor the points of push and pull where the higher mind is concerned. However, as you shift from one feeling into another, you may wish to keep your mind clear as your emotions flush through the lower feelings of fear.

When we resist change we experience harshness, but when we surrender to change, our awakening period is accelerated. I first heard the statement, "When you say yes to God and take one step forward, God will always take 100 steps toward you." As I continue to move through my own form of clearing, this deeper knowing is always reassuring. In emotional/mental terms this means that as you learn to allow rather than push against the energy of your emotions, you are trusting God enough to let go and allow yourself to feel the old wounds and in doing so, this letting go of what was will accelerate the clearing process.

You may ask during this time of intense change, "How do I get through to the mind more clearly?" The answer? Ask. This form of asking is in actuality a command. You are commanding your higher self forth for greatest and highest expression by asking the mind to fully release and transmute all lower vibration to Light.

You can liken this process to the dissolve technique in movies. As the director wishes to transition from one scene into another, she dissolves the first scene into the beginning of another for building the story from beginning to end. It is the same with the communication of higher mind to soul. You are asking that you hear directly from Source by commanding it to be so.

With practice, you will begin to notice a shift in consciousness, your confidence levels will rise, or you will physically feel it in your body. The shift is usually accompanied by a bit of laughter to find that you have merely claimed more of who you are. This form of shaping your reality is a positive ritual on a daily basis and one that, over time, will prove itself invaluable as you dissolve from being afraid of the world to sailing on the winds of change in your life.

We are all One, yet have come into this world to experience the many facets of God's creation. Fear is not a vibration that resonates with the higher realms of consciousness. An ocean knows no difference in the many creatures that inhabit its water, yet there are numerous temperature zones and levels of alkalinity in which they reside.

The vastness of the world's oceans can be seen only from outer space. From this perspective we gain a true understanding of what form and shape it takes. Evolving from sea creatures to land walkers, our lives seem overwhelming as we adjust to solid ground. It's only when we stop to gain perspective that we can take a step back and breathe a deep sigh of relief.

Suspend all judgment

All beings have their time of pushing into the newness of life, and a time for resting to take in the vastness of all that has come before them. This feeling can be likened to collapsing into a heap of restfulness after taking a strenuous hike up a mountainside. There is nothing wrong with coming to rest and there is nothing wrong with the great wanderings of heart. Learning takes all shapes, all forms and there is no right or wrong in any choice.

It is merely a process of learning. It is *all* learning. The view and experience is different but both have value and merit. If there is judgment in either, it is in what has come before you or what is about to come after. It may be that the person who is currently soaring in their soul learning chose to rest just before launch. Conversely another may have just completed a major developmental phase and is now choosing to rest.

A sure sign of judgment can be found in any form of internal, mindful rule making. These are the rules that dictate. "If it happens to me, it is to happen to you also." This idea is to say that you are the same as another, and if you are not, then there is something wrong with the other person with no thought of looking within. Just remember that, not only are we one body, mind and one Spirit, we are also walking talking, electromagnetic fields that change with every thought, feeling and behavior.

When you are directing the feeling of judgment toward another, then the effect of this vibration is not only felt by the receiver but also by you, the sender. As you honor yourself, you honor others. Conversely, if you harbor thoughts of ill will, schemes of demise or judgment toward another, then in essence you are condemning yourself. Be true to the old adage, "Do unto others as ye would have done to you."

As we recognize that all worlds are one and that we are all interconnected, we will realize that what happens to one, happens to everyone and everything. Anger directed at any perceived enemy only comes back to hit you right where you live, in your home with your family but also reverberates in your body.

One such situation is unfolding in our world today. The United States of America was struck by a terrible attack on its World Trade Center on September 11, 2001. We responded by empowering our government to hunt down the perpetrators. As months turned into years, our collective grief turned into rage. The United States then waged war on a sovereign nation. We are now in the midst killing and being killed by others for the sake of funneling our hatred at one man who we had decided was the root of all evil. It was hate and rage that first set this cycle of aggression and retaliation into motion, and it is rage and anger that continues to feed the fires of fear. When will the cycle be broken?

As both participants and armchair critics, we can only guess how devastating our actions will finally be played out. After watching the steady stream of images and hear the reports flow into

171

our living rooms, our emotions will continue to churn from the prolonged violence. Many lives have already been turned upside down, but no one is ever spared the pain and agony of this type of lower vibrational learning. One person's villain is always another's inner reflection of the self.

We are one body, one mind and one heart, all pulsating and creating as the same body of universal life force. There is no difference or greater importance in one aspect of humanity than another. You are in total command of your world and accountable for your thoughts, words and deeds.

You may ask how this applies to the terrible things that are happening in the world today. Where there is war, hatred, discontent or undesirable living conditions, you might say, "I would never create what is happening in the world today. I would choose differently."

The solution is simple but takes practice and perseverance. Change and transform yourself, and everything else will also change. This is a basic theory of Quantum mechanics. Researchers have come to call it the God principle because they have witnessed the phenomenon of matter changing while at a completely separate location without any interference, its counter part also changes. Austrian scientists recently demonstrated this in an experiment that resulted in a single fulleren molecule, composed of a sphere of 60 carbon atoms that spontaneously appeared in two places at once. Following this logic, when a critical mass of people shift into a higher consciousness or higher vibratory pattern, the whole of humanity will also shift into the same frequency.

Take total responsibility for everything you create about your life

Most assuredly when you reach a high state of peace you will realize nothing at all matters within the realm of comparisons. It is not the mind of rule making that says, "do it this way to gain, to access, to experience," but the kind of rule making that says, "if you do *not* do it this way you will feel the consequences of your wronged behavior" that suppresses, not only our inner Light but especially our children."

Humankind uses judgment to parent children all the time. It is the way most of us were brought up, which is bending their Spirit to get them to focus on their mind. Yet, there is another way that honors the child as a fellow spiritual being of Light.

We are all leaders in the new world consciousness. We have only to listen to the prompting of our soul that leads us to our heart's desire.

The parent can bend or surrender *their* mind to the greater will of God to honor the Spirit of the child. As a parent myself, I cannot say with all my heart that I have fully surrendered to this God centered way of nurturing, but I recognize the profound impact I have had on the life of my own two children as I bent their will for the sake of conformity.

Even when we are in need of disciplining a child, respect of the individual, no matter what age or stage of learning is to be honored at all times. When we lash out in fear or anger, we not only hurt the child, but their spirit as well.

I found that when I did not behave in a way that fit the situation or acted out of fear and ignorance, I would find myself in

173

a state of anguish later. As I stumbled my way through my role as a single parent, it was always clear in hindsight when I needed to apologize for my unknowing. Over time, this learning curve with my children was profoundly healing and liberating as we worked together to realize that we are all in this life together.

The veil of understanding is always lifted after an intense period of learning. If you are open, your Guides will show you the convoluted ways of your path to self-discovery that will seem almost humorous at times. As you realize that you are not seeing beyond your current veil of understanding, you must trust, simply trust and your heart will lead the way.

Shifting into joy breaks this closed cycle of learning. If you have consciously chosen the spiritual path, you have without question chosen to realize joy. God is the frequency of love and love unites even the most broken of hearts. You will have come home to God when you have taken the high road in all areas of your life. When you have put the pieces of your soul fragments back together and healed, you will release yourself from the bondage of duality.

You are not the limitations and disenfranchised circumstances that your mind wishes to believe. Bypass the mind and go straight to Source. Only then will the higher mind serve to open your heart. May you be so very blessed in your life's adventure as I feel myself to be. There is encouragement all around you, and there is no tomorrow like today. It does not matter what your age, weight, height, or emotional predisposition is. It only takes the courage to take that first step by asking why and why not? Keep asking until you get the answers that satisfies your soul.

Taking responsibility for what you create is what matters most. Where issues of the heart are concerned, there is no second best. You are a divine being who is in the midst of a human experience. Everything you think, feel and do affects your soul's journey toward union with the ultimate in divine creation.

When this occurs, it is as if you have fallen in love with life and have no stops, no confinements, no handicaps, no boundaries. Life is what you choose it to be. But this is no armchair choosing. This choice comes with taking total responsibly for absolutely every emotion that is invoked with each step you take. This may be hard to swallow hook, line and sinker as the mind moves from victimhood to empowerment, perpetrator to awareness level holder. In all of creation, there is no truth that dictates *less than* behavior or holds you or anyone else down to experiencing thought patterns rooted in fear.

You may choose to believe you are somehow less than Divine but it does not make it so. If you would like to check yourself against this basic principle, allow your mind to wander into some aspect of your life you are wishing to be different. In this replaying of life, you will find buried beneath the rubble, a belief that led you to determine your current situation, circumstance or state of mind. Prior to this time did you ever consciously say to your soul, "Bring me unhappiness, dissatisfaction?" Yet you are a product of that very belief. You may believe that someone or something may have put you there, but is this really true?

If you answered yes, then you have bought into a self-limiting belief. In reality no one can put you anywhere, push you into doing anything or force you to do anything you have not already given them permission to do.

I am not saying that we consciously will harsh lessons upon ourselves but I am saying that by our own ignorance, we sometimes give our power away by unconsciously acting out of fear because of who we believe ourselves to be. We are powerful beings of Light.

Everything you do and everywhere you turn, you are facing aspects of your own divinity. You are leaving clues every moment of every day. You can be both very happy and satisfied with these aspects of yourself, or not. This again is where choice comes into play.

The most productive way to change your outside world is to first change by opening your heart to a greater acceptance of yourself and others. When the inner changes, the outer must also change. There is no other alternative.

Making way for change is the biggest challenge. It requires your full attention to the details of your life. If you are to become truly happy then you must give of yourself freely to others and know that in this giving there is a wellspring of joy there to supply all the energy needed to carry forth your own personal brand of passion into the world.

Giving of yourself accelerates the manifestation of your innermost desires. You may get very frustrated if you have taken on the belief that self-giving means you surrender your inner Light so that others can shine or you feel that by putting your desires first you are selfish. In actuality, it is the other way around. If you do *not* put yourself first you are dishonoring your soul's passion for awakening. I am not advising you to feel no compassion for others, but before you can offer kindness to another, you must first know how it feels to be kind to yourself.

If you believe it means to give of your time, talents and earnings to the point of hurting or suppressing yourself, this type of giving not only hurts yourself but the very individuals you are trying to help. This misidentified feeling of compassion is another form of *less than* living.

Your choice in your physical life expression is to discover your own brand of joy and share this feeling with others. The very nature of joy brings forth a swelling of enthusiasm and emotional release. Joy is the essential ingredient for realizing your heart's desire. All who make the shift from complacency to activation of their heart's desire become spiritual warriors because they command their higher Light into physical expression.

Even as you realize that your path is a spiritual one, you will find yourself perpetually on the path of self-destruction, but with practice it will become easier to identify the pitfalls. As soon as you find yourself falling into the lower trap of emoting, stop your thoughts and get recentered in heart where you can then discern your misguided behavior. In the still point of creation, release your self-doubting belief and correct your path from that of self-destruction to self-empowerment.

This is not necessarily a painless process. Sometimes it may take you into an emotional whirlwind of turbulence to get your mind to settle back into a state of calm. Once you recognize what misidentified belief is holding you back, you are then called to release it and embrace the part of yourself that you have alienated. These are the times when the ego tends to jump up and shout at the mind to do something to protect turf and territory. Acknowledge it as a lovely light, embrace your human nature, then reassure yourself that you are the divine being in charge of your creation.

The mind wants war and vengeance while the heart desires peace through the act of surrender. Depending on the nudging from the soul, the personality self will intend one way or another.

You will find in your quest to free yourself from fear, this scenario will be played out many times, many ways throughout your life. You may see each situation differently, but in essence you are a powerful being of Light fully and completely in charge of your soul's journey.

Once you begin discovering your gifts from Spirit, joy will become more and more a part of your day instead of the occasion. As you more fully transition into the higher vibrations, you will begin to experience not only an increased level of satisfaction in life, you will also find yourself stepping differently as you transform patterns into the reality of the dream you hold in your heart.

Your personality self knows nothing of the larger picture and will only sense a resistance to whatever adversity you may be up against. During times of physical struggle when the body is under attack, the mind is either holding steady or is in complete alignment with Source. Of course, there are subtleties and degrees in-between.

You will pick up on the clues from the soul who ultimately has the last word in the decision. However, the higher mind is deciding on the breath of intrinsic learning the soul has decided to accomplish just prior to the incarnation. This is when the mind will persevere or will begin to send signals to you that it is time to release the body. On the ground level, we experience this as our inner will to survive or to give up on life altogether.

The beauty of the personality self is when it connects directly to the soul and either bypasses the higher mind altogether or harmonizes with the mind to become one stream of energetic Light.

Break the tie to the body-mind connection

The reasons why the body expires from life is not a surprise to the medical community and there is much less research on the soul in the mix of this reasoning. There are many theories that fully support the interplay between free will and one's autonomic system, but the Guides tell me it is the soul's choice that ultimately drives the physical functioning of the body.

I once listened to a taped interview of a man tell his story of dying on an operating table and coming back to life three days later. He and his wife were on a spiritual quest to see Sai Baba. The man fell ill and was rushed to the hospital where doctors worked on him to no avail. As his body failed, he felt himself slip up and out of his body. Once fully out, he

Each cycle of change calls us to more fully embrace the wholeness of who we are. By calling forth our higher vibrational frequencies, we claim our birthrights.

was no longer in pain and continued to watch the doctors and nurses working on him with fascination.

At first, he worried about all the things he was leaving behind, but then as his concern decreased, he found himself in what he described as a hall of souls. With Sai Baba at his side, another soul read a long list of his many lives to see what he had realized in his learning. He was then told that he had prematurely left the body and was given the choice to return. He thought about it, then finally decided to go back so he could be with his wife.

Just then, he found himself waking up in what felt like a cesspool of a body. The hospital had been so short handed, they had put his broken corpse in a closed storage room after stuffing cotton

179

up his nose and in his ears. He said he started screaming for someone to come and help him. When the hospital staff discovered the commotion they were understandably in a state of shock. It took him months to recover from the ailments of the body but he had full recall and was able to tell others exactly what had happened.

Even with such a dramatic way of gaining such knowledge, that we are not the body and that we have full choice whether to stay or go from the physical world, it is very difficult to disassociate our minds from the physical vessel. After all it is the facade of life in our three dimensional reality that drives us to survive. We would recognize our loved ones no matter what form they were to take as long as their vibratory patterns remain within the core essence of who they are. We are not the mind-body connection, yet we relish our physical surroundings. The physical world allows us to experience our emotions in a more visceral way than in a disincarnate or ethereal state of being.

Just as we have chosen our primary resonance, our angels and Guides have also chosen theirs. We are all one and are experiencing life together.

Life in the flow of higher vibratory patterns can be quite magical and almost surreal at times. I have often wondered if my children are aware of the iridescent glow of light and love that surrounds them now, the same as when they were very young. Youth brings forth the newness of life. As you grow into your awakenings, it is not necessary to move through the stages of disillusionment, but it takes the most dedicated spiritual seeker to transcend the illusions of fear. I cannot tell you a sure fire way to stay up and out of the fray of the emotions, but I do feel that with due diligence, life improves and changes as we gain a deeper level of understanding.

Some days you may be very *up* when life is moving along. This is when you are experiencing a tremendous amount of joy and satisfaction, then you will come into a space and recognize that your emotions have dampened. You may experience this up and down process for a moment, a day or until you experience another 'aha' moment. When you do, your mood swings back to a higher feeling of joy and your awareness is heightened. In this state of being, a new opportunity will arise or possibly a relationship that was stuck will break open.

As you continue to traverse your path to freedom, you will find many obstacles that will present themselves, but it is all a matter of choice to fight and deny the change or to surrender your fears to God. The reactionary part of yourself will automatically want to recoil in fear, while the higher mind fights off the perceived threat and backs away from the challenge to change or ponders what action to take. This is where daily prayer and meditation will smooth the way. As you incorporate the connecting linkages between the personality and the higher self, the mountains will become valleys and a deep dark pit of despair will become a pothole in the road of life.

RESENTMENT AND ANGER

Letting go of anger and resentment is the key to freedom, to peace of mind.

In order to love your God with all, your everything, you must center yourself within the Divine Light and become one with it.

Attachment to your friends, your family, even to your self as you identify, must merge with the one God essence of love. Give your all, your everything to God.

Live your life in complete knowledge that all is well. Everything is in accordance with God's plan. You have only to recognize this reality as the essence of your existence. All else will follow.

Only after you have truly recognized this as truth, will you be at peace.

All judgment, opinions, accusations, angers, resentments, frustrations and jealousies will fall, will melt away, and become only a distant remembrance of something of another mode of life.

All that will remain is the knowingness of divine will and love. Everything will be seen through the eyes of love and adoration for all of creation.

Everything happens according to Divine will. Know this is so and rejoice in this knowledge.

To love, to love all in creation, is Divine.

To rise above your human pettiness of emotion and strife is the key to true happiness. Therefore, there is no reason for resentment or anger.

You will begin to understand that the things that

have happened in your life are put there only
to help you to see who you really are.

Do not hold onto those lessons of the past.
They are only there to teach.
Let them go and you will be free.

Look at everything as a stepping stone to the
Divine.

Always keep in mind where you are and
where you want to be.

You are to keep your focus firmly planted
on God, and what is God but love.

Please love.

Love all. Love freely, give freely without
thought...and rejoice.

—August 7, 1991
Sri Sathya Sai Baba

WHY DOES LOVE ESCAPE ME?

Guides: Love is the answer to any given question and questions come in all forms. From humanity's primordial scream to know God to the cry for love from another, humankind has misidentified love as fear. It can be said that humanity has become lost in a sea of discontent.

As long as humankind lives in fear we shall not fully know and understand the true nature of Divinity. God's love is unconditional and comes without malice, judgment or qualification. It is gentle and kind, generous in all its sweetness. Love is the essence of humankind's existence.

Your internal dialogue might sound like mine.

> *So why does love escape me? I refuse to listen to my heart. If only I could quiet my mind, I could hear my heart tell me the answer. All the answers to life's questions would come in the quiet of the night, full of promise and hope.*

> *Oh, why do I not listen? I am afraid. I am afraid to trust my heart but I know it speaks truth. I'm afraid that I might get my heart's desire. If I do, I will be forced to accept happiness to the fullest extent of God's promise. This will force me to give up power, lust, greed, control; doubt of all promises unbroken. If I trust in my heart's direction, then I will be free. With freedom comes responsibility.*
> *Am I prepared?*

OPENING TO LOVE

I feel deeply depressed.
I have leapt into the void, followed my heart and
I hurt.

I'm afraid.
I'm afraid to reach but I have.

All of my unworthiness has resurfaced.
I'm afraid of the pain, the hurt.
It hurts to love someone and not be loved in return.

The risk that one must take to reach, to give, to keep
one's heart open even if it hurts.

The wounds have not fully healed.
The fear has resurfaced.
It is here with me trying to overtake me.

You have leapt into the void and must simply trust.
You are always to trust, to have faith.
You are well protected in my Light of love.

Living life is in the doing.
That's all that matters.
It is all in the doing.

You must live your life in every moment.
To follow your heart.
To reach out and to give freely.
For you know that I will always protect you.

Without chances there is no adventure.
To love, to reach, to reach for love,
Simply *be* love;

For all of humanity and yourself, you are loved.

—*June 14, 1991*
Sri Sathya Sai Baba

*A human being is a part of the whole called by us
universe, a part limited in time and space.*

*He experiences himself, his thoughts and
feelings as something separated from the rest, a
kind of optical delusion of his consciousness.*

*This delusion is a kind of prison for us, restrict-
ing us to our personal desires and to affection for
a few persons nearest to us.*

*Our task must be to free ourselves from this
prison by widening our circle of
compassion to embrace all living
creatures and the whole of nature in its beauty.*

—Albert Einstein

CHAPTER SIX

REVERBERATIONS AS WE TRANSITION

*Clearing the channel between the lower parts
of self to make way for the entirety of the soul to
descend will take an act of courageousness,
but we are ready.*

What the stages are and how to identify them

There are many kinds of awakenings of heart and only awareness is required to garner our attention. We sway and swoon over the idea of change. We are enamored with the beings of Light who guide us to our freedom, but rarely do we recognize that we are all there is. *We are the beings of Light.* We are all One and we are that which we desire to know and to understand. Knowing and being this Love that we are is our birthright.

The world of fear is no match for love to be sure, but we are always identifying with our limitations and rarely do we allow ourselves to feel and to be that which we already are. Many souls come into this realm of being and continuously slip back into denying the very source of their creation. It is like a fish forgetting it can swim. The very source of our creation is love, yet we forget and begin to pretend that we are something that we are not.

The transition stages, while residing in the Source of your creation, are very different than when you are steeped in the roadblocks of the mind. The feeling of being in "Source" requires that you quiet the mind as you encounter the many facets of change. God will challenge you to transform from a belief in fear so that you can begin to identify with, and more fully merge with, the Love that you are.

Only God fully knows the many pathways into your hearts of hearts. Your job is simply to trust. With patience, you will make your way through the maze of learning to listen to your heart and begin to discover the outward manifestations of your innermost desires. You will identify it as a heightened sense of personal well-being. If you have still been resisting the allowance of Spirit in your life up to this point on some level, just remember to relax and trust that you are where you need to be in the cycle of change.

By this stage, you have transitioned from being overcome by fear and living in a reactionary cycle of life happenings to recognizing and releasing the patterns that have so held you captive. If you are at this state in the transition from fear to joy, then the following guidance will help you gain a footing into paying attention to the subtleties of the prompts from Spirit.

Just remember that it is all about learning to listen to your heart rather than reacting to the mind. As you gain experience, your connection and emergence with Source will provide you with the sense of peace that will stand the test of any assault on your senses.

The higher mind, as said previously, will get in the way of the heart. So the question must be asked, how do you override the roar of the higher mind when the heart is speaking quietly, softly?

When life seems to be moving along at a pretty fast pace and with many distractions, there is little incentive to go within for the answers that plague this part of your emotional-mental make-up. Once you have surrendered to a joyful way of living, of listening to your inner knowing, it does not then mean that you are home free. The many fears that you initially overcame to get to a place of peace will resurface time and time again, but in different forms, until you have fully cleared them from your energy bodies.

The higher mind takes time to reprogram to accept the leadership of your heart. It helps if you learn to see the heart and mind as if they are two separate, living, breathing aspects of your being that are to come into greater harmony and balance.

You can intend that the heart and mind work together for the purpose of realizing and actualizing your innermost desires. This is where the higher mind is best called into service, after the realization of oneness with all that is and before the heart has fully opened wide to Source. Therein lies the making of a true partnership and union in Spirit.

The mind carries with it the autonomic intellect and reasoning powers, while the heart center is linked to your feelings and is tuned to the vibration of Love. In the still point where the higher mind calms to a state of neutral, the two now meet and merge as one. You have accepted the challenge of the soul to transform the lower feelings of fear into higher frequencies of Love, and have recognized that a greater degree of cooperation with the higher mind is needed.

At this point, on the personality level, you are registering the will of the soul and, by doing so, your soul pushes energy into your auric field to make another shift.

In your day-to-day awareness you may find this very disconcerting because you will feel the higher vibrations of energy on the physical level as common ailments such as flu symptoms, colds, allergies or sinus drainage. Your body will also register the shifts as aches and pains, sharp pin-prick type sensations on the feet, legs and arms, head and back areas. Vertigo and nausea will also come and go. Emotionally, you may process the release of your lower emotions, held in your subconscious by your higher mind, as depression, melancholy or loss of energy.

Your sleep cycle may also be interrupted and dreams may occur to be strangely laced with seemingly past-life occurrences or other worldly lessons occurring before the mind's eye. At times you may also experience death-like feelings and melancholy that have absolutely no relation to your mood or expression up until this point in your shifting phase.

You may also experience a sharp high-pitched buzzing kind of noise in your inner hearing or hear a single or plurality of voices. Patterns of imagery or ghost-like figures that appear from out of nowhere may be disconcerting, but simply remain in a neutral state of watchfulness.

As you begin to shift from being motivated by the ego into a deeper state of being in heart, it is not uncommon to meld into time and space warp kind of feelings of other worlds. Literally you are now moving into other worlds. If you register fear, you will be snapped back into the third dimensional reality of earth stratosphere. That is O.K. and just consider it a part of the learning process.

As you learn to accept without judgment or qualification, your whole world will begin to open up. The angelic realms will become quite clear at times and telepathic communication is so very enjoyable and delightful. The spirit world resonates as a high vibration of joy. The many spirit beings will help you raise your awareness to theirs, and as you do so, the veil will be lifted.

You can maintain this heightened state of being as you incorporate the frequencies of energy into your auric field. To do so requires that you ground them into the physical body. This occurs best by taking concrete steps to honor the prompts from your soul by honoring your truth.

As you continue to ground the higher lightwave frequencies into your physical expression, you will experience a greater sense of joy and light-heartedness that is more akin to the angelic realms. This process is an ongoing one, and one that will bring much satisfaction as you accelerate the release of the many layers of heaviness.

As you more fully surrender to the process of change, you will find that your physical discomfort lessens. Depending on just how attached you are to the beliefs that no longer serve you, you will experience these phenomena at length or just briefly. Your willingness to surrender to this part of your clearing determines your acceptance level of God's healing. When called to do so, affirm your conviction by saying something like, "Yes. I surrender to the highest expression of who I am, and so be it."

Even as you begin to more fully understand the spiritual principles at work in your life, you may, at this stage in your development cycle, decide to remain steady or continue the ascension process. This is a very delicate time in your learning and one that warrants wise decision-making. There is no mercy in the fields of vision and when the sight is fully activated, your understanding may not yet be in place to go with it.

You are on the spiritual path simply because you are a spiritual being having a human experience, but as you start working to bring a greater degree of peace and feeling of oneness into your life, you will seek to understand everything that is being put before you. Yet, no one has schooled you in the kind of awakenings you are invoking by your mere willingness to come to know your true self.

The same analogy that applies to spiritual self-discoveries is the same as it is in everyday life. For instance, someone who has just returned from an exotic island may try to tell what the trip might be like for you. They can tell you about their journey. Then you set out upon your own travels and discover an entirely different place.

Your spiritual awakenings are the same. You will experience your learning in your own unique way. As you move through the process of lifting the veil, just call on your guides and ask the hard questions. For instance, as your energy bodies begin to open, you may ask, "what do I do when my awareness dramatically shifts?"

The things you know as a physically operational adult in your world of street corners and office buildings may be turned upside down as you experience wayward entities gliding in and out of your field of vision. When strange phenomena occur, who do you turn to, what questions do you ask? If you are not careful, someone will think you are crazy.

Where there is a will, there is always a method for solving the most basic mysteries. You will find individuals who are experiencing similar phenomenon who have acquainted themselves with the ways of the universe. It is a different orientation from the everyday physical reality. This orientation requires that you let go of everything you may have believed about the structure between the Creator and creation.

When you suddenly find that your senses have opened up to include deeper levels of perception, you may feel a bit over-whelmed at first. You may have been used to depending on a very limited channel to discern the world around you, but suddenly you discover there is much more to reality than previously experienced.

The gifts of Spirit can be quite a natural occurrence if you are willing to keep an open mind. With each new experience, and as your perception of your expanded reality opens up, just keep asking your Guides for explanation and clarification.

As the lines between the physical boundaries disappear, you may suddenly find yourself thinking of someone then hear from them or decide to call someone out of the blue only to hear that they had just been thinking about you. A deeper level of tuning into thought is occurring and you are responding by hearing what someone is thinking before they say it.

You have your own inner conflicts to work through, and the learning is accelerated when you begin to more acutely sense what others are thinking and feeling. It will call you to look at your own inner conflicts. It takes time to fine-tune the ability to screen out the many thought patterns of others. You may also take a while to discern what you are to tune into and what you are to leave alone.

This first starting occurring when I was still working on a project that was very political in nature. It was not uncommon for the management team to hold meetings in private, decide a group strategy then take their ideas into a larger meeting. I began to notice, especially during strategy sessions, that I

193

responded more to what someone was thinking rather than to what they were actually saying. The disparity between the two was often jarring.

Over time, I discovered what was happening and decided that every outside thought, *everything,* was to be tuned out. Now, I am focused only on what is going on with *me*, and not getting distracted by anything else. This may help you enormously with filtering out any confusion as you adjust to the many changes underway.

As your senses open up to this way of communicating, be sure to maintain a sense of balance and peace as you honor the spiritual law of non-interference.

During this unfolding process, someone may tell you what to expect, but you will experience the learning as if you are a pioneer discovering virgin territory. You must experience the altered states of reality to truly understand the ramifications of the many layers and levels of the universal life force on earth. No one else can do this for you. You may quickly come to realize that there is much more to your world of oneness than meets the limited spectrum of the naked eye.

Science has most certainly proved this by the invention of telescopes and microscopes for seeing into the worlds that are limited by normal sight. How often would one have to adjust an ultra ray gun or 'tele-psychic' instrument for the purpose of tuning in and gaining access to the larger spectrum beyond our five senses and perceptions.

The most wondrous experience that has served to open my eyes was when I first started seeing people for who they really are. I would hear their worries and concerns as they were working through difficult lessons, yet experience the intensity of their Light as angelic beings. The contrast between what they were feeling and who they actually are is astounding. *All of us* are the angel-like beings who have taken form as chiropractors, doctors, stay-at-home moms, school attendants, teachers of children, wayward street-corner holders, everyone.

I once saw a gigantic tall warrior of Light that looked like something out of a science-fiction movie walking down the street near the train station in Fredericksburg. I have since seen him around town. This very strong and very powerful Light warrior is in direct contrast to the physical form of a hunched-over man who was pushing an empty shopping cart the day I first saw him. This opened my eyes to the understanding that we are never to make judgments about or against anyone. We are here to experience our humanness as the Divine in whatever form we have chosen.

As you work through your most intense times of shifting, you are to keep your focus on what is going on inside of you to more adeptly adjust to the many forms of change as you move through them. There is no one set way of experiencing vibrational shifting.

Since we live in a physical world, we are bound to experience the change in the body at some point or another. I have learned to equate these sometimes-strange bodily symptoms with the release process and have sought out some unconventional types of treatments and modalities for helping me to throw off the lower emotional debris as they are released from my energy fields.

We are also creatures of comfort. In times that the body is transitioning from one vibrational frequency into another, pay close attention to what you are feeling to discern what is needed to bring the body, mind and spirit into full alignment with Source.

During any release process, you will benefit by keeping your spirits high and your body moving. Below you will find a sample list of some ideas that may help:

1   A more active physical workout
2. Daily prayer and meditation
3. Change in routine
4. The good company of a spiritually focused friend
5. Career and relationship guidance
6. Body work and energetic healing
7. Chiropractic to properly align the spine
8. Physical checkup by a trained medical professional who is attuned to listening to the more subtle signs of change in body chemistry and linking symptoms to thought wave patterns
9. Personal transformational workshops
10. Bypassing the mind-body connection all together with light or sound therapy
11. More play, more fun in your life all around

The list can be as long and as varied as the need arises. As you grow into the higher lights of understanding and leave the last vestiges of fear-driven living behind, you will find the wide world of love united in Spirit to be a fascinating adventure.

As you transition more fully into joyful awakenings, there will come a time when you may feel that life as you have been living it will just not suffice. The Guides tell me that approximately 53 percent of all spiritual seekers feel this way. Suddenly the lives they have created up to a certain point in time are just no longer working for them. They want more change, faster and intend it to be so. By following your soul's commanding of your life into a different state of being, you will begin to feel discontent, unhappy with your present set of circumstances, restlessness or a strong desire to change your environment.

At the point where you not only recognize this state of being, but are ready to do something about it, your soul channels a big push of energy into your auric field. When this occurs you may experience a disruption in your way of living including your relationships and living conditions or you may suddenly feel a general sense of boredom with what you have created. Life in the physical will begin to change radically, depending on how much shifting is needed to realign yourself with your soul's higher expression.

Our choice to stay or to leave the physical body influences our decision to let go of fear.

You will find that this way of being catapults you into a vital part of your transition as you begin to sense the changes ahead. Any life transition is a challenge, but where your soul is calling you to transform, you will receive the inner prompting long before the actual occurrence. You may wish to ignore it, but the feeling of impending change is unmistakable.

An example of this kind of shifting occurred in my own life during the summer of 2001. I was going through an unusually intense period of energetic clearing and was feeling an overpowering feeling of pressure of energy coming into my body, to the point that I was physically hurting. I had been feeling this way off and on for months, but this time was different. Just as I was feeling compelled to stop my workday because I could no longer contend with the pain, a friend called. With my concentration down to zero, she suggested that I take a hot salt bath as a possible remedy.

197

As I remained in the silence of the moment, an overpowering crush of energy pushed into my body, and as it did, I felt the conscious part of myself rising up and out of the physical to escape the excruciating pain. I was leaving my body and thought I was literally going to die. I verbally called out to the universe that I needed help, right now.

Just as I got out of the tub to dry off, another friend called to say, "I'd like to give you a Reiki treatment, but you have to come to my office *right now*."

I quickly got dressed and jumped in my car. On the way to her office, I cried, not from the excruciating pain, but from a feeling of profound awe at having received such a direct response from God. When I arrived and came within only a few feet of her, I immediately felt the need to get sick.

She worked on me for over two hours that day stabilizing my auric field. I felt that my left side was on fire while my right side was almost normal. My head felt as though it would explode from the pain. Throughout the session, we both realized that I was in the midst of permanently leaving my body. She kept willing me to stay. At one critical point, she called out to me, which snapped me out of my resolve to escape the pain. I was well out of the body following that energetic silver cord (that tethers each of us to the physical) I had followed so many times before. As she continued to work with me, I willed myself to come back.

This particular event became so dramatic because I had been ignoring the prompting of my guides for months and months. They were trying to get me to redirect my life in ways that are only now becoming self-evident. My life path that day took a major turn toward realizing my soul's highest expression, but at the time, I just wanted to escape the pain.

Just a few weeks after that dramatic episode, I decided to stop ignoring the inner prompt to go see Mark Torgeson, a massage therapist and gifted composer/pianist, I had met at a seminar in the spring of the year. Two days prior to attending the workshop, I was given that I would meet a man that would become very important to me. Since he was only one of two men in the room that day, and I already knew the other one, it was pretty obvious which one my guides were talking about.

This same friend who worked to bring me back into balance had also organized the session and had been trading professional services with him. Throughout the summer, she kept reminding me of my vision, and that I needed to go see him. I just didn't want to; I was busy building the organization I mentioned earlier. It finally took this drastic experience and a patrol officer ticketing me just outside his office door to get me to take action. I finally picked up the phone and made an appointment.

Just a short two weeks later, I was visiting this same friend's house enjoying a lazy Sunday afternoon at poolside with my kids and others. The prompt from Spirit actually happened quite suddenly when, in the middle of the visit, I felt a huge inner push to leave. It wasn't the kind of gentle reminder or prompt that said, "leave soon." No. This was, "leave *right now.*"

Just two days before, he had invited me to join him for a spiritual retreat in the Virginia mountains. I categorically dismissed the invite because I had already accepted the opportunity to visit with friends. Promptly at 3:00 p.m. that afternoon, in the middle of conversation, a panic came over me with instructions entering as a voice in my mind that said, "go to the mountains."

I abruptly left the gathering, drove home, threw some basic provisions in my car and headed west. I didn't know where

I was going, exactly, but when I finally got there it was after dark. With not even moonlight to guide me, the way up was pitch black. I could not see in front of my face. As I fumbled my way up the rocky trail, the only flashlight I thought to bring, a penlight, kept cutting out. With that panic feeling still within me, at first I decided I would just sit down and wait until morning, but then decided to continue the climb. I arrived at my destination in a drench of sweat with my lungs feeling as though they would burst from the stiff walk and fear of loosing my way.

From the first time I stepped up onto the wooden deck of this mountain retreat and cleared my mind, I went into a deeply altered state where the veil fully lifted. Over the next few days, as I walked through a glen of trees, I heard the chatter of Mother Nature. I learned about the structure of God's natural kingdom from the rocks and trees that hold the consciousness of evolution. I knew when the trees started talking to me that I had pierced the veil of my very limited understanding.

While in this surreal feeling where time becomes fluid, I decided that I was either loosing my grip on reality altogether or that there was more to consciousness than the beliefs I held so dear. I was immersed in an expanded reality that to this day is still within me.

I have found that, with every new experience, once the channel is opened, there is no going back. Each time I allow myself to relax and merge with the God within, I am there, in that energy, and become fully immersed in the grand play of God's kingdom.

For me to more fully awaken to my divine expression, it took a series of dramas caused by ignoring the prompts from my guides to change before my life became so harsh and the drama I had created took over. In my life, my soul took drastic measure to get me to pay attention and begin breaking through the many self-imposed mind created roadblocks. I had such a history of ignoring or denying my inner guidance that it finally took this impending choice of permanently leaving my body that I decided to stay.

Our higher selves will use whatever method to get each of us to our intended rendezvous point, but this does not mean that when we are finally tuning in that we are home free. No, it does not. It simply means the 'aha' moments don't have to be so dramatic or painful.

Since that short time ago, I have been working through many of the same doubts and indecisions I have experienced my whole life, but from a different perspective and with less intensity. Now, I experience many more days of happiness and exhilaration and fewer languishing in the doldrums of fear and self-doubt.

In spiritual terms, there is no stronger action than setting an intention. Consciously choosing how you will fulfill your heart's desire will put the wheels of change into high gear. As you do so, you will be faced with the beliefs that are no longer serving you. These deeply rooted beliefs will come up for release and take form as memories laced with dark, sad or disturbing emotions. If you find yourself immersed in scenarios and mulling over old events or emotions; stop it. Just will yourself to stop this moving picture that invokes such lower resonances as guilt, shame, remorse, regret and hurt. Stop the emoting, and affirm that you are choosing differently now.

Remember the intent you first set as you affirmed your resolve to release yourself from fear. Bless the knowing that came from these old expressions and release your emotional attachment to them. As you put this new way of creating inner peace into practice and learn to transcend the inner doubts and insecurities

201

about living life in this new way, your transition from the old way of mulling over emotion and the strategy of intending your higher expression will quicken your awakening.

As you begin transitioning into fulfilling your heart's desire, the blocks of the higher mind will become easier to spot with a dose of willingness. It is only through your constant mantra of surrender to the Divine that true change will come about. Otherwise, you will seek out seemingly safe and secure choices, but you are actually settling into complacency. Once again, it is O.K. to intend a resting-place to stop along the way, to take pause and enjoy the journey—just be clear that you are intending so out of joy.

However you decide to experience your journey of self-discovery, it is wise to always remind yourself to keep your focus in the moment. As you practice this, you will find that your intrinsic experience becomes a more peaceful one.

When you have come to the point of recognizing that you are being called to take a more active role in your awakening by serving the greater good, it will not come as a surprise. For most, it is a feeling that has been with us from birth. This call to serve is already deep within us. At this stage, your soul will provoke you to more fully recognize who you are.

For others who are still steeped in fear, who have yet to reach this stage of self-discovery, your joyous and open-hearted nature act as an advertisement for positive change. You, like many others, are now wishing to embrace the best that life has to offer.

As you have come to this point of decision, it is not that you are unwilling to work hard for what you desire, but you are now moving through a process of eliminating what you *do not* desire. As explained in chapter four, the process of eliminating secondary beliefs that hold you back from realizing your highest expression will be played out as you continue to experience less than optimal outcomes. For example, if you are holding onto a belief of being separate from God, even as you declare your highest nature to be love reunited with Spirit, you may still be manifesting less than what you desire. Know that it is merely a learning process and don't be hard on yourself. Be O.K. and affirm your heart's desire as you acknowledge your learning.

The earth is shifting in vibrational frequencies just as we are. In fact, the entire world as we know it will not be the same 10 years from now.

The spirit world is closely aligned with the more subtle energy found in nature. You can learn a lot about humanity by immersing yourself in its wonderment, which is always in balance and harmony. It is very difficult to feel separate and apart from the higher realms when you are looking at a beautiful butterfly alight on a sunny morning in July. The devas are fluttering right along side the bounties of nature and have come to say that all is in balance and right with life, if you will just stop and listen to what God's kingdom is sharing with you.

You are a creator and a part of the magnificence of this kingdom. You cannot forget this fact amidst nature in such balance and harmony. The butterfly is a perfect teacher. Just as the caterpillar morphs into this most wondrous creature of Light, you, too, metamorphose into your higher self by reaching for your heart's desire. Like a caterpillar in a cocoon, you, too, go within to discover the true beauty hidden there. This giving side of your human nature serves you well when you are unsure of the changing forces of nature as you move through your time here on earth.

Where your human family is concerned, there are many who would doubt the validity of spiritual matters in life's awakenings, but it is true that you can clear the air where the heart is concerned. It is a joyous life serving others. It is a violation of divine law to surrender your Light to another, for the sake of safety and well being or any other reason.

Your future is full of promise and hope if you ignite the passions within you. If you sit idle in fear or complacency, you are not only dishonoring those who have come before you but have also destroyed your future hopes of discovering the very nature of your divinity incarnate in the physical expression of life.

You cannot fully surrender the beliefs that block you from realizing your bliss, unless or until you have merged with the divine nature of who you are. Your soul calls out to you for the change you have intended, and you have only to recognize your true nature.

How do you maintain these inner feelings of belonging to the greater humanity when you are in the mode of transitioning from one current of vibration into another? It is a matter of putting your focus on God and constantly surrounding yourself with a sea of white Light, the divine essence of who you are. You are indeed a divine being who is here to transform your vibrational frequency from lower into higher, but you must keep your focus on your goal of surrendering to the will of God each day. Upon rising you may wish to repeat these words, "I am that I am. I am God incarnate in physicality." These now familiar few words, when said with conviction, seat your soul more fully into your physical expression.

As you progress through your day, continually remind yourself of who you are. I have found this is best accomplished by maintaining a humble stance of prayer. This prayer is one that is said with meaning and conviction.

Many who have been brought up in traditional forms of ritual worship are familiar with this feeling of saying a most sacred prayer or mantra without any form of heart based feeling. As you command the God being that you are, remind yourself that the greater will of God is in charge each day.

As you practice this ritual with heartfelt determination, you are literally commanding the higher vibrations that you are to be fully present. This does not mean that you are taking a back seat to what is being put before you. You are fully engaged in the adventure. You cannot possibly call on your soul to fully incarnate in the physical and not become a full participant in your own creation without conviction. It is not possible any other way.

However, many spiritual seekers get to a particular point in their journey and grow tired of always being on the ready. Many wait for others to come along and help, or wish their way into the kingdom of heaven.

Indeed, the kingdom of heaven is right here on earth. Each day that you awaken affords you the opportunity to create your wildest dreams and your most cherished memories. It is the stuff that brings you back to this way of living time and time and time again. On the soul level, some enjoy the journey of life in the physical and learning so much that they repeat the same learning over and over and over again.

This type of learning becomes ingrained in our intrinsic nature, but can also wreak havoc on our energy bodies. It is always a risk to repeat lessons so many times because, every time the veil is lifted after the end of each lifetime, we are forever reminded of how sweet the ride of life is.

However, after each feeling of exhilaration over what we have learned, the veil then comes back down as a shroud covering our Light, and there we go again immersed in yet another life of learning. Souls can become so enmeshed in the learning that they forget their mission of transcending fear. If we are not careful, this way of learning can become a part of who we are. By doing so, we begin to buy into the fact that we are that which we have created rather than absorbing the intrinsic learning and not the baggage that goes along with it.

The good news is that now we are in a time where we can choose to integrate higher vibrations of energy consciously while still in the body. The Guides tell me that the last time this higher Light was made available to mass consciousness was in the year 1213. At that time there was an earth shifting that lasted a millennium and will not end until the year 2013. It was during this time in our history that mankind was not prepared to accept the higher Light in the physical but, instead, was motivated to ascend to the higher realms in other ways.

An example of this can be found in the recorded history of the Crusades. There is suggestion in the annals of history that an act of mass ascension took place about this time. It involved 50,000 children who willingly left their homes to follow the will of God. This expedition called the Children's Crusade began in the year 1212 about the time of Easter and Pentecost. Without anyone having preached or called for it and prompted by who knows what, many thousands of boys, ranging in age from six years to full maturity, left their plows or carts they were driving, the flocks they were pasturing, and anything else they were doing and joined the Crusade. They did this despite the wishes of their parents, relatives and friends who called after them to turn back.

Suddenly, one ran after another to take up the cross. By groups of twenty, fifty or a hundred, they put up banners and began a journey to Jerusalem. Many people asked them who had urged them to set out upon this path. They were asked especially since only a few years earlier many kings, many great dukes, and people of powerful stature had gone there and returned in defeat.

The bands of children were not strong enough or powerful enough to do anything. Everyone, therefore, judged them foolish for trying to do this. They briefly replied that they were equal to the Divine will in this matter and that, whatever God might wish to do with them, they would accept it willingly and with humble spirit. They made little progress on their journey. Some were turned back at Metz, others at Piacenza, and others even at Rome. No one knows exactly what happened to them because only a few returned.

A few years later, this same higher Light was the push that took form as the Magna Carta. This document is often thought of as the cornerstone of liberty and the chief defense against arbitrary and unjust rule in England. In fact, it contains few sweeping statements of principle, but is a series of concessions wrung from the unwilling King John by his rebellious barons in 1215. However fragmented humankind was at that time, the Magna Carta, established for the first time, a very significant constitutional principle, namely that the power of the king could be limited by a written grant.

The Guides tell us that there is an overlap of consciousness between 1213 and 2013, and represents a dimensional shift in mass consciousness as well. There are many overlaying dimensions that are in simultaneous construction, and this is just one of them.

They say that just as strange that 50,000 children would willingly leave their homes to follow the will of God, we may see, at times, many souls descending into the earth plane in a way that is foreign to our current orientation to our physical life. This prophesied shift in mass consciousness is not to interfere with our ability to see clearly. We can use past world events as a different way of seeing to better understand what is coming. The way to maintain our equilibrium during these upcoming times is to remain fully present and to keep our focused awareness in the moment of our experiences.

The Guides tell us that in the year 2013, these various layers of mass consciousness will once again merge. It is as if half of humanity went into a shift during the year 1213 and continued on its course of divided learning, while another part continued on a course to realize higher realms of peace, joy and love. Soon all of humanity will come together again.

What does this different way of seeing have to do with reverberations as you shift in consciousness? Your ability to see and to discern what is best and doable for your immediate future as you ascend into higher states of awareness and joy is determined by your willingness to let go of fear-laden beliefs that no longer serve you. Humankind has often chosen the path of limited vision through our learning in past lives, past centuries. It is not uncommon to pick this way of lesson-giving as most admirable and as an accelerated way to ascend to the higher Lights of understanding.

"There shall come a time on the physical earth that the paradise our forefathers have dreamt of shall come about. We shall be there also in this paradise that we call home. Be there now, and hold that energy of home in your heart. Know it is true, and we shall be there with all of humanity."

—*Carol Fitzpatrick,* excerpt from "Songs and Stories of Creation,"

teachings of the Divine Masters

AFFIRMING FAITH

I have chosen.
I have chosen my path.
My path has been set.

I follow the path of Light.
He is my Light, my protector, my teacher.
I follow the path of enlightenment.
I strive to illuminate my soul.

Liberation is my goal.

The path has been steep and treacherous.
The fear has been overpowering at times.

There still are valleys, but I know I am safe in
his arms.

He is there with me always,
encouraging me along the way.
I delight in God's Love.

—June 12, 1991

AWARENESS OPENS DOOR TO LIGHT

Awareness brings hope. Hope is the intrinsic nature of God. God is all knowing.

As souls determine their path of righteousness, there is Light that surrounds them and lifts their journey from one that is rooted in struggle to one that is soldiered into joy. Joy breeds happiness among those wishing to understand the nature of God, for God brings awareness of thought, word and deed. It is the deed of awareness that opens and connects all souls to God.

It is your Father's good pleasure
to give you the Kingdom.

—Luke 12:32

CHAPTER SEVEN

FREEDOM DRAWS NEAR

Learning to play as the creators that we are takes patience with our human nature.

Tapping into Joy

You are a spiritual warrior now with a cause, but have yet to actualize your dream of fulfilling your heart's desire and have become quite familiar with manifesting secondary desires and releasing them. As the grip of fear is relinquished and you awaken more fully to your soul's calling, you will begin to realize that you are truly a creator of your own reality, but remiss may still be plaguing you.

With freedom in sight, it is now time to relinquish the many thought forms that have gotten you into this kind of trouble to begin with. As you open up to experience a greater degree of freedom, you may also realize that you are free from the constraints of having to fulfill someone else's desire as they too have a right to fulfill what they see for themselves.

It may take you a very long time to discover this, but when you do it is very exciting and also scary because you realize that you know how to play by someone else's rules but not necessarily by your own. This feeling inside of you, to fully break free from the last vestiges of self-imposed constraints, is a growing anticipation of what is coming.

213

During the first stages of your freedom seeking, you may try to find someone to fulfill it for you. At first this seems to be a pretty good strategy, because it is similar to what you have known before. You can experience the freedom while holding yourself safe while others actualize your desire.

However, the day will come when you realize that if you are to have your heart's desire fulfilled, you must fulfill it yourself. This is really scary at first, but then you think about it. It's not so scary as you look around and find others doing really expansive things with their lives and loving every minute of it.

As you think about it some more, you will realize that not only can you realize your heart's desire, but you also may not be so bogged down with nagging worry. You may think that once you get going again, you might get stuck in the muck and mire of worry and doubt, then have to take a back seat or even get lost and have to go play by someone else's rules again. Your heart's desire though does not work that way.

Create your own rules or have no rules at all

Once you jump into the river of joy, so to speak, you are in a very different environment and one that requires you to sink, swim or relax and float your way through life. Whichever way you pick, you are now in a different current, a different river.

It is time to tackle the nuances of moving from a very receptive form of clearing to one that requires that you become a participant instead of a recipient. This clearing to remove lower debris, or the more subtle beliefs that no longer serve you, requires you to take action.

Once you recognize your heart's desire and have done much of your clearing work, you will move into a phase of development that signals to the higher self, "I am ready."

"Ready for what?" you might ask. This question is key because for as long as you can remember, you have played by someone else's rules. These are the *get along at all costs* kind of rules that dictate your very belief in survival. But now you are fully aware of your divine nature and you have chosen to live as the soul in the physical world around you. This is quite a different stance than merely doing what it takes to take care of yourself and keep a roof over your head.

You may be much more fortunate than this basic principle of survival, but it is the very foundational belief that keeps you from leaping from one form of living fully into another.

Many who have already traversed this path are pioneers in our time. These are not necessarily the individuals who have amassed piles of money from working long hard hours or from the stock market, for instance. These individuals are still toiling away and have still bought into the belief that money and all its trappings bring security, happiness and fulfillment. This is only a small part of what brings the heart joy and creates a sense of abundance. You cannot remember who you are when you are immersed in the river of illusionary forces. No matter how secure you feel, these are worldly forces that keep you bound by fear not by joy.

Choose freedom over enslavement

If you remain rooted in the illusions of the physical, you will never understand Jesus who taught that a rich man cannot get through the eye of a needle to reach heaven, but a poor one can simply walk through the gates at will. This parable is meant to teach the difference between illusion and reality. Material abundance is not a bad thing, as long as you keep your focus. Mother Teresa gave her monetary award from winning the Nobel Peace Prize to her efforts in India.

Align with what fuels your passion for realizing joy and as you do so, you will adjoin with others who are also gathering in these higher vibratory patterns. By doing so, you are aligning your personal will with the greater will of God. A time will come when the lower vibratory patterns will experience a quickening to merge with the higher.

If you find yourself working against the current of the greater Will, your energy centers will be zapped and the longer you continue, you will feel drained of the very life force that feeds your soul. This is counter intuitive and is not a part of the reality you are choosing.

This is not the kind of suppression that monitors your every move, but one that calls out to the adventure and spirit of the moment with every day, in every way.

The greatest joy is one of service

When you are in a state of repose, your energy bodies are forever seeking new vibratory patterns. When this occurs you may sometimes feel as though you may explode energetically. This phenomenon is short lived and is the result of your auric field merging with the greater cosmos. It is as if you are literally connecting with all that is.

While in this feeling of oneness, you may find that your perception of time begin to shift. As you begin to live more fully in the moment of your experiences, your focus will more dramatically change from past and future to simply present. You can perpetuate this feeling by calling forth the universal love of God and immerse yourself in this state of being everyday until it becomes you, not simply something you are striving for.

There are many universes and galaxies of Spirit that are also experiencing this form of expansive awakening. It is the creative spark within all that unites us in thought, word and deed.

The ultimate goal of humankind is to bring our hearts into alignment with all that is. The means to do so is right here within us. We can feel it.

Once we realize the vastness of God's kingdom and that each infinitesimal detail of our lives is also in divine order, we can more peacefully merge into the oneness. Conversely, this is true for everyone who has been born into a system of governance that says, "we the people" that takes the actual form of *we know what is best.*

In actuality, we are all leaders of our own destiny, and we are also collectively tied together. There is no trace of fear in this divine system of governance.

It is as if we are travelling down the river of love on innertubes all tied together. We are each having our own unique experience, yet we are all there together. Such is the way with humanity. We are all connected, while individually expressing joy as we create our own unique experience.

As you have now realized your own way of experiencing peace and love from the Divine it is also timely that you begin to more fully express your own unique brand of exhilaration. There is only one rule of thumb to follow. Don't hold back.

217

Give it everything you've got. You are the star in your own play. Enjoy the feeling of creation, practice it to the fullest extent, then go out there and express, create, celebrate and enjoy the laughter. It only lasts a lifetime, and it is good. You have only to follow your heart, and all else will unfold before you in a synchronistic kaleidoscope kind of wondrous, magical way.

FREEDOM

Guides: Freedom is an elusive word used to describe many a hero's welcome home. It is home which we are enamored. Freedom comes when home is realized. For when we are in Source all souls are home. God's home is safety, comfort, love, joy, blissfulness, ecstasy of the Beloved.

All souls wish to return to Source for home symbolizes creation. Creation is the symbol of family.

I am a creation of the Divine. Glory to the mother, father God of creation and all the children. Behold freedom draws near.

Soft sweet speech is the expression
of genuine Love.
Hate screeches, fear squeals,
conceit trumpets,
but love sings lullabies;
it soothes, it applies balm.
Practice the vocabulary of love.

—Sathya Sai Baba

CLOSING THOUGHTS

About the learning

Writing this book has been one of the most rewarding times in my life, but it has also been one of the most challenging because, as Spirit would have it, this past year has also served as one of the most introspective. As the project comes to close, I am very thankful that I feel myself 'back in my body again.' I have worked diligently to more fully integrate and ground the higher vibrations of Light into the physical realities of my life. This more grounded feeling has come about because I finally assumed full responsibility for choosing my current path. It has not been easy to break away from what I felt was a more socially acceptable path, but by learning to trust my inner voice of reason more than the outer view of what is occurring in the world around me, I am finally coming to terms with how I am being called to to manifest my heart's desire.

Through the process of writing and clearing, I have discovered that my highest expression or primary heart's desire is to share joy, and more joy! This expression has taken form as a partnership with gifted composer/musician Mark Torgeson called *Songs and Stories of Creation*.

While listening to Mark's spontaneously composed music, I see, hear and feel the many stories of creation played out before me. As my mind moves into a state of neutral, I am accessing encoded knowledge embedded in the musical intonations. As the veil is more fully lifted and as Spirit directs, I am shown prophesy, or future probabilities, of entire regions, cultures and peoples. I have come to share these foretellings in parable-like stories for the sake of shifting mass consciousness.

Within each story, participants begin to understand the power of One as they are called to say 'yes' to embrace and to accept a greater degree of joy, love and peace into their lives. Through the musical tones and patterns of speaking, Spirit also directs specific Light wave frequencies into the light bodies of those who are open and willing to receive God's grace for healing and transformation. It is quite magnificent and humbling to see God's handiwork in our lives.

After months of immersing myself in the work, I have come to understand that humanity is currently playing out approximately seventeen and a half future probabilities. The Guides have shown me so many things about where we have come from and where we are going, but they have also made it clear that we (humanity as a whole in part, and part in whole) are the ones in charge of shaping our final destination. The angels and guides are here to help, but we are the ones who must choose, then lead the way.

We can deny our very God like qualities and sit in the doldrums of doubt and fear, or we can embrace our birthright as spiritual beings of Light and ascend to the higher realms of understanding. The choice is fully ours to make. What will you choose?

In closing, I honor and celebrate the Light that you are, and wish for you, a most wondrous feeling of joy, and more joy!

Just as the world can reveal itself as particles,
the Tao can reveal itself as human beings.

Though world and particles aren't the same,
neither are they different.

Though the cosmic body and your body aren't the same,
neither are they different.

World and particles, bodies and beings,
time and space;

All are transient expressions of the Tao.
Unseeable, ungraspable, the Tao is beyond any attempt
to analyze or categorize it.

At the same time,
its truth is everywhere you turn.

If you can let go of it with your mind
and surround it with your heart,
it will live inside you forever.

—The Teachings of Lao Tzu

———————————

Thank you Guides!
...and the many angelic beings
of Light in my life.

———————————

223

Quick Order Form

- **Fax orders**: 540-786-4853. Send this form.

- **Telephone orders:** Call 540.785-7770.
  Have your credit card ready.

- **Email orders:** carol@carolynnfitzpatrick.com

- **Postal orders:** Community Works!, PO Box 41132
  Fredericksburg, VA 22404, Fredericksburg, VA 22404, USA.
  Telephone: 540-785-7770.

Please send more FREE information on:
- ❏ Other Books/CDs
- ❏ Speaking/Seminars
- ❏ Upcoming Events
- ❏ Consulting
- ❏ Mailing lists (receive an electronic and/or postal newsletter)

Name: _____

Address: _____

City:_____State:_____Zip: _____

Telephone:_____

Email address: _____

Sales tax: Please add 4.5% for products shipped to Virginia addresses.

Shipping by air:
U.S.: $4.000 for first book or disk and $2.00 for each additional product.

International: $9.00 for first book or disk; $5.00 for each additional product (estimate).

Payment: ❏ Cheque ❏ Credit Card:
          ❏ Visa   ❏ Mastercard   ❏ AMEX   ❏ Discover

Card number:_____

Name on card:_____ Exp. date: _____

Number of Books _____ x $15.95 = _____

Sales Tax (if applicable)   _____

Shipping   _____

TOTAL   _____